49 WAYS TO WRITE YOURSELF WELL

JACKEE HOLDER

49 WAYS TO
WRITE
YOURSELF WELL

The science and wisdom of writing and journaling

JACKEE HOLDER

step
beach

First published in Great Britain in 2013 by Step Beach Press Ltd, Brighton

A CIP catalogue record for this title is available from the British Library.

ISBN 978 1 908779 07 6

Picture credits

p17 Joe Shlabotnik; p22 Sharron Wallace; p38 Ruthanne Reid; pp35, 43, 63, 124 Jackee Holder; p56, 57 Labyrinthos Photo Library – www.labyrinthos.net; p58 Naomi Sachs, Therapeutic Landscapes Network; p68 D Sharon Pruitt; pp53, 70, 123 Robin Rezende; p76 Beatrice Murch; p82 flickr.com/photosteve101; p97 Kevin Dooley; p105 Surian Soosay; p109 Vladimir Fofanov; p110 Stephanie Dale; p114 Tax credits; p124 Holly Kuchera; p127 Mihai Tamasila; p142 Jen Morgan

Series editor Jan Alcoe

Edited by Grace Fairley

Typeset in Brighton, UK by Keren Turner at Katch Creative

Cover design by Keren Turner at Katch Creative

Printed and bound by Star Standard Industries, Singapore

Step Beach Press Ltd, 28 Osborne Villas, Hove, East Sussex BN3 2RE

www.stepbeachpress.co.uk

For all my paper mentors from the early years to 2012 – thank you.

Acknowledgements

This is a thank you to those individuals in my life who have knowingly and unknowingly, positively contributed to me getting this book written. I am deeply grateful.

Jan Alcoe

Aida Campbell Holder

Sharron Wallace

Suzette Clough

Nina Grunfeld

Martha Holder

Eric Maisel

John McConnel

Sandra Parris

Jo Hathaway

Grace Fairley

Keren Turner

49 Ways to Well-being Series

If you have selected this book, you may be looking for practical ways of improving your well-being. If you are a health and well-being practitioner or therapist, you may be helping your clients to improve theirs by encouraging them to practise some of the approaches it is based on. Well-being is a subjective state of 'feeling good' which has physical, mental, emotional and even spiritual dimensions.

Because these dimensions overlap and interact, it is possible to improve well-being by making positive changes in any one of them. For example, taking up regular exercise (a focus on physical well-being) may improve concentration (mental well-being), happiness (emotional well-being) and sense of purpose (spiritual well-being). This series of well-being books is designed to provide a variety of routes to recovering, sustaining, protecting and enhancing well-being, depending on your interests and motivations. While some emphasise psychological techniques, others are based on physical movement, nutrition, journaling and many other approaches.

Each book in the series provides 49 practical ways of improving well-being, based on a particular therapeutic approach and written by an expert in that field. Based on tried and tested approaches, each title offers the user a rich source of tools for well-being. Some of these can be used effectively for improving general resilience; others are particularly helpful for specific problems or issues you may be dealing with, for example, recovering from illness, improving relaxation and sleep, or boosting motivation and self-confidence.

Enjoy dipping into any *49 Ways* book and selecting ones which catch your interest or help you to meet a need at a particular time. We have deliberately included many different ideas for practice, knowing that some will be more appropriate at different times, in different situations and with different individuals. You may find certain approaches so helpful or enjoyable that you build them into everyday living, as part of your own well-being strategy.

Having explored one book, you may be interested in using some of the other titles to add to your well-being 'toolbox', learning how to approach your well-being via a number of different therapeutic routes.

For more information about the series, including current and forthcoming titles, visit **www.stepbeachpress.co.uk/well-being**

CONTENTS

1 2 3 4 5 6 7 8
9 10 11 12 13 14
15 16 17 18 19
20 21 22 23 24
25 26 27 28 29
30 31 32 33 34
35 36 37 38 39
40 41 42 43 44
45 46 47 48 49

INTRODUCTION

Welcome to *49 Ways to Write Yourself Well*. As you explore this guide, you will be learning about and using a wide range of ideas and techniques to improve your well-being, drawn from the broad fields of creativity, contemporary psychology, psychotherapy, journal and writing therapy, coaching, personal development, neuro-linguistic programming (NLP) and sometimes plain common sense. The practices and content have been sourced from research into the therapeutic benefits and value of writing and the strong links between our thinking, emotions and behaviour. By sharing some of the research, science and kitchen-table wisdom behind the therapeutic benefits of creative writing, the book shows you how writing can help you gain a deeper and more creative understanding of yourself and what really matters to you.

This guide will steer you around the pitfalls of negative thinking, managing difficult emotions and stress-led behaviours that have an impact on your physical, emotional and mental well-being. You'll learn how to use writing as your own self-therapy, offering insights into your inner life. You will draw on your own creative resources in positive ways to explore your thoughts and feelings, your relationship with yourself and others, and how writing can help you discover yourself in simple and significant ways. You'll discover how writing can help you find answers and solutions to your own questions and how establishing a regular writing habit will guide you towards what is real and important to you.

By the end of the book, you'll be confident to take to the page, write wholeheartedly about your feelings and emotions and use a range of models and techniques to help you with any difficulties or challenges you may be experiencing in your life or at work. Writing is a journey of discovery and you'll be surprised by what is revealed by the imprint of your hand moving across the page, day after day.

WHO THE BOOK IS AIMED AT

This book is written for health care practitioners and the people they work with, and for anyone interested in gaining a better understanding of themselves using writing as a tool. If you're a clinician, therapist, facilitator or group leader, you will find this a rich resource for the people you work with and a reflective and reflexive resource for yourself. We're on dangerous territory when we do not take the same medicine we prescribe to others. Try out the writing practices in your own journal or notebook and you'll be able to offer others a deeper understanding of the practices based on your own experience.

Perhaps you're new to journaling or you're returning to it after a long break. Or maybe you think, as many of us have told ourselves, 'I'm just no good at this writing thing'. Don't worry. Many of the foundations suggested at the beginning of the book for establishing your writing practice will set you free from the fear of grammar and perfection. The good news is that not all of the practices require writing. Some invite you to play and use drawing and imagery in your journals and notebooks, and you don't need to be a Picasso or Rembrandt to do this.

THE 49 WAYS

Each numbered 'way' provides a simple route to recovering, preserving or enhancing your well-being through the process of writing. It will usually include:

- underpinning theory, research, evidence or information on how writing can help and how to use it for your own therapeutic benefits
- a '**Write now**' longer writing or creativity practice to put the theories or models to work on the page
- a '**Tip**' is sometimes included to offer more information or something else you can try
- '**See also**', which suggests other numbered 'ways' that you may find it helpful to look at.

At the back of the book you will find key references, so you can find out more about subjects that interest you.

The 49 Ways are organised into chapters, each with a different focus. Here is a summary of the main chapters.

CHAPTER BY CHAPTER

Chapter 1: Getting Started: Establishing a writing practice to write yourself well

This chapter introduces you to the nuts and bolts of setting up your writing practice. This is the one chapter you are encouraged to read in a linear form. Once you are past these early pages, you are free to roam and move through the book in your own time and at your own rhythm. Writing is a practice that requires regularity and focused attention, like taking a yoga or tai chi class and this chapter will help you establish your own practice and systems that will help you to write on a regular basis. It introduces you to the reasons for keeping a journal or notebook and why writing first thing in the morning really does work for many individuals. It covers where and how to write, and establishing the best places and spots that work for you. It introduces the methods of free writing and morning pages*, shows you how to establish your writing rituals and habits, and guides you in creating and using your own collection of writing and visual prompts.

The chapter ends with you meeting and connecting with your 'inner wise writing self'* and grounding the practices that will support your writing, as well as a centring practice that you can use at the start or close of any of the writing sessions you engage in. These practices underpin the contents and spirit of this book and the cultivation of a more healing writing practice. Learning to embody these practices will enable you to grow and know yourself through writing, and to gain from the healing benefits writing will bring to you and your well-being.

Chapter 2: Escape the Digital: Why writing by hand with pen and paper works

This chapter looks at why writing by hand makes a difference and explores creative ways of engaging with your journals and notebooks. The digital world is rapidly taking the place of the ancient tradition of writing by hand. This chapter outlines some of the benefits of writing by hand and how it differs from writing with a keyboard and computer. You will discover the benefits of writing with your non-dominant hand* and how to use it to gain and mine your own inner wisdom. By connecting with the messages and language of your non-dominant hand* you can try out the 'Write now' practice of identifying your inner animal by using both the dominant and non-dominant

hands*. You will have fun drawing and discover how drawing in your journals and notebooks can improve your observational abilities and allow you to sit more in the present moment. You will learn how drawing or using images can capture the language that words on a page sometimes miss. You can also practise taking a problem or challenge on a writing walk on the page through the sacred ritual of 'walking the labyrinth'.

Chapter 3: Managing Your Emotions: How to write for emotional balance

How we respond to our emotions can be a blueprint for our everyday actions and behaviours. Emotions can sometimes feel overwhelming but you will learn that it is more rewarding to face your emotions than take flight. This chapter will help you gain a better understanding of how emotions work and offer practical ways of handling emotions and beliefs that get in the way of your emotional, mental and often physical well-being. It will take you through identifying your specific moods, flushing out those core beliefs and identifying ways to give your emotional life balance through the 'Write now' practices. This chapter ends with a look at intuition* and how developing this sixth sense can help create a better you and help you make better choices and decisions by using your intuitive intelligence.

Chapter 4: Therapy on the Page: Therapeutic models to challenge your thoughts and beliefs

There is much to be gained from traditional therapy that will help you gain insights into yourself. This chapter combines powerful techniques from psychology, therapy and coaching and introduces therapeutic

models and theories that you can use quickly to process and gain insights into your relationships with others and your own actions and behaviours. With regular practice, alongside your free writing and morning pages*, you will build and develop your own inner wise writing self* as you gain greater perspective on your relationships with yourself and others.

Each of the 'Write now' practices in this chapter shows you, the 'author', how to take charge of your own learning and growth by embedding these techniques as writing practices that will become second nature to you.

You will be shown how to use the rational emotive behavioural therapy ABCDE model to confront your beliefs if you are experiencing self-doubt or a lack of confidence. Not sure what impact positive and negative words hold in writing? This chapter will teach you about research that highlights the importance of

balance in the use of negative and positive words when writing about traumatic events. Having a conflict with a colleague or family member? The chapter explores the neuro-linguistic programming (NLP) model of perceptual positions. You will learn about life scripts, drivers and the Karpman Drama Triangle*, all of which are models and theories originating from transactional analysis work.

The chapter ends with a focus on a set of transformational questions that you can try out on yourself to self-coach your way from problem to solution. This chapter will help you to better understand the dynamic and interpersonal relationships between you and others and between others and yourself, and interpersonal communication in groups in both formal and informal settings.

Chapter 5: Writing Therapy: Change the script!
How often have you felt, 'If I could only change my life story'? Well now you can, by applying

some of the techniques and approaches of narrative therapists Michael White and David Epston. Much of the content of this chapter has been inspired by the real possibilities that narrative therapy* offers you to re-author your life story. By engaging in the 'Write now' practices in this chapter you will learn how to re-author and reframe your own life experiences on the page. Rather than settle for 'This happened to me', you will learn how to reframe and rewrite your story to give it your own meaning.

This chapter shows how fiction writing can create a 'safe enough' distance between you and your life experiences to allow you to achieve a different and useful perspective on your own life story. We take a look at forgiveness and how writing about forgiveness brings its own healing and benefits, how to make best use of your perceived failures and how to transform them on the page. The chapter ends by considering how writing can help you to 'unpack' your personal history and your relationship with money, on the page.

Chapter 6: Nature Wisdom, Body Wisdom and Writing Wisdom

Nature has always been an inspiration for writers and this chapter opens up a space for you to explore your own relationship with nature, as a writer. It highlights the very important connection between nature and writing. Research and studies repeatedly confirm the many health and psychological benefits of being with nature. With this in mind, the idea of walking is explored and reveals how walking as a practice is a valuable activity for deepening our well-being and practice as writers. And there's nothing like a bit of poetry to ground you in nature and walking so we explore the value of poetry and how to use

it for therapeutic purposes. We then move in to explore the body through the senses, along with exploring the psychological and health benefits of starting a 'gratitude journal' and cultivating a 'gratitude practice'. The final 'ways' aim to rekindle the almost lost art of personal letter writing by encouraging you to write letters to your younger and older selves. The chapter closes with a ritual to bring your writing journey to a place of genuine acknowledgement and appreciation.

GLOSSARY
There is a glossary at the back of this book, which explains some of the terms used in the text. Any word or words that appear in the glossary have an asterisk next to them in the text, like this*.

USEFUL RESOURCES
Finally, I have listed some 'writing prescriptions', a personal list of recommendations of writing and healing books.

While you can start using the ideas and activities in this book in any order, I would encourage you to begin with the 'Getting started' practices in Chapter 1. These are designed to set up your writing practice and get you going. Beyond that, please use this book in any way that most appeals and is helpful to you, working through it chronologically or dipping in and out, and finding your own 'flow' through the exercises.

Many of the techniques introduced in this book work most effectively when you pause and give yourself the time and space to write without expectation or judgment. Whilst the book is structured with the 'Write now' practices, you have complete permission to go off topic at any point of your writing, with any of the suggested activities. This book is about writing from your heart and the mystery of the writing process alone determines that, most of the time, this route cannot be prescribed.

Whilst the health and psychological benefits of writing are becoming clearer to us, the greatest wisdom lies in your moving your hand across the page, daily, weekly or as often as is realistically possible. Your repeated mining of your own lived and felt experience will reveal to you, often in the most unexpected ways, the wisdom of your writing and what it has to say to you, when you allow yourself to be open to what emerges. Not only will you gain from many of the psychological and physical benefits writing offers but you will also gain from accessing your own inner wisdom.

WHAT YOU'LL NEED FOR YOUR WRITING JOURNEY

The key essentials for your writing toolkit are a pen, pencil and collection of crayons, colouring pencils or felt tips (pencils can be freeing and easy to write with and take us back to times as a child) and a notebook. You'll need a couple of your favourite pens. Find pens that are light and easy to use or that write quickly and smoothly. It's not essential to have a computer; in fact, we'd much prefer you do as much writing as possible by hand.

Ideally, have in your possession a couple of blank notebooks in which to record your responses from each of the chapters as you work through them. It's a good idea to date each entry and include the chapter number, so you can cross-reference when you read back through your notes.

A NOTE OF WARNING

Many of the exercises in this book could trigger and put you in touch with strong emotions. Some emotions may emerge from painful or difficult experiences from your past that you may not feel equipped with to deal with on your own. While writing therapy can and is effective with working through emotions it is not to be used to address trauma or significant physical, emotional or mental health problems. If feelings arise that feel overwhelming, please seek appropriate medical and professional help or support. It's a good idea to have a friend or family member you can trust who can be contacted at short notice and with whom you can talk things through.

We would suggest that this is essential if you are experiencing any of the following:

- undiagnosed pain, physical symptoms or sleep problems
- symptoms of depression, such as loss of motivation, loss of appetite, changes in sleeping habits, persistent negative thinking
- high levels of anxiety or anger or recurring panic attacks
- substance misuse or self-harming behaviours
- social isolation due to severe lack of confidence or self-esteem
- persistent relationship difficulties.

EMOTIONAL RELEASE

Be prepared for some expression of your emotions as you work through the book, so you'll need a packet of tissues. At some point, and I cannot say when, your own journey will determine that you'll shed a tear. Tears are good. I once heard that there are 20 toxins released in each teardrop. The poet Robert Frost (1949) declared, '*No tears in the writer, no tears in the reader*'.

I imagine that many of you may have fears and concerns or doubts about the cans of worms your writing may open up. Writing in this way is on many levels letting go of control. You may connect with unfamiliar parts of yourself that survive underneath the surface. Writing, if you allow it to, will take you below the surface. If left to its own devices it will bring unexpected tears but it will also clear the way for better, more informed understanding. It will shake things up – but in a good way. I encourage you to stay with it. In her book, *Write Yourself*, Gillie Bolton (2011) shares, '*People do cry at their writing. Handled well and sensitively, these are healing tears.*'

I hope you enjoy your writing journey and inner explorations.

1 2 3 4 5 6 7 8
9 10 11 12 13 14
15 16 17 18 19
20 21 22 23 24
25 26 27 28 29
30 31 32 33 34
35 36 37 38 39
40 41 42 43 44
45 46 47 48 49

Chapter 1

GETTING STARTED: ESTABLISHING A WRITING PRACTICE TO WRITE YOURSELF WELL

This chapter introduces you to the nuts and bolts of setting up your writing practice. This is the one chapter you are encouraged to read in a linear form. Once you are past these early pages, you are free to roam and move through the book in your own time and at your own rhythm. Writing is a practice that requires regularity and focused attention, like taking a yoga or tai chi class and this chapter will help you establish your own practice and systems that will help you to write on a regular basis. It introduces you to the reasons for keeping a journal or notebook and why writing first thing in the morning really does work for many individuals. It covers where and how to write, and establishing the best places and spots that work for you. It introduces the methods of free writing and morning pages*, shows you how to establish your writing rituals and habits, and guides you in creating and using your own collection of writing and visual prompts.

The chapter ends with you meeting and connecting with your 'inner wise writing self'* and grounding the practices that will support your writing, as well as a centring practice that you can use at the start or close of any of the writing sessions you engage in. These practices underpin the contents and spirit of this book and the cultivation of a more healing writing practice. Learning to embody these practices will enable you to grow and know yourself through writing and to gain from the healing benefits writing will bring to you and your well-being.

WAY 1

Journal writing and notebooks

'Paper and pen are endlessly patient, present and never make a comment.'
Gillie Bolton, 2011 (consultant in reflective writing)

JOURNAL THERAPY

Journal therapy is the practice of writing down your thoughts as a way to make sense of them and come to a better understanding of yourself and the issues you are experiencing.

The roots of journal therapy stem from the work of the psychologist Dr Ira Progoff, psychotherapist Christina Baldwin and expert in journal writing Tristine Rainer. Dr Progoff was instrumental in the early development of journal therapy after recognising that his clients were able to achieve outcomes rapidly by writing about their experiences.

By keeping a journal or notebook, you're doing a number of things at the same time that will bring you therapeutic benefit as well as personal fulfilment:

- It's a way of focusing your life and extracting what is meaningful.
- Writing is evidence that you exist outside your roles and the job you do.
- It slows you down and gives you space to be more mindful.
- It's an inexpensive way of getting troublesome or worrying thoughts out of your head and onto the page.

- Through a regular practice of writing, you'll discover new things and be surprised.
- People who journal experience higher levels of self-awareness and are able to reduce their anxiety levels.
- Journaling allows you to view situations from a different perspective.
- It's an objective space that won't judge you, where you can capture the good, the difficult and whatever sits between the two.
- Journaling has been proven to have both psychological and physical benefits. (You'll find more about the research findings later on in the book.)
- It helps you to identify what you really want and create ways of reaching your goals.
- It prevents you from projecting unresolved issues onto others.
- It allows you to make connections with your inner, wiser self.
- It's a great way of getting to know yourself better.

Even though this book lays out guidelines for keeping a journal or notebook, you can essentially write about anything you want. You can whine and moan, or write about the weather or what you had for dinner, as it's for your eyes only. It's safe to write down your thoughts about someone that would be upsetting to tell them face to face. Equally, it's the ideal space to capture a quote that lifts your spirits or an idea that you want to develop.

Quotes that resonate

1. Poet Susan Goldsmith Wooldridge (1996) says about her journal writing, '*I'm free inside myself to create my idea of beauty or mess up. I explain with no one watching and it keeps me alive.*'

2. Author and creative genius Sark (2008) writes, '*I love journal keeping because it has helped me to discover and uncover myself, to encourage my own bravery, sort out difficulties with other people, to invent new ways of being.*'

3. International freelance consultant in therapeutic writing and reflective practice

Gillie Bolton (2011) believes that, '*Writing is actually a process of deep listening, attending to some of the many voices in the self that are habitually blanketed during our waking lives.*'

Strong and powerful words, don't you think? Which of the above quotes most resonates with you? Perhaps you'd like to scribble down your thoughts and reflections in your journal or notebook as your first 'Write now' practice, to get you started.

Write now

Tip: Your notebook is special. It's an extension of you and is to be handled with care. By this, I mean taking care of your notebooks is an extension of taking care of you. So treat your notebook well and know that it's about to become a delightful laboratory, holding in its pages true reflections and recordings of who you really are and who you're about to become.

CHOOSING YOUR JOURNAL

There is no need for fancy equipment and you won't be required to go to any great expense. For your journey, you'll need a couple of notebooks for your writing. It's up to you whether you call it a journal or a notebook. You'll be using your journal or notebook to record your responses to the 'Write now' writing practices contained within these pages, and to capture your reflections, observations and ideas that emerge from any of the practices outlined in the book.

Your notebook is your personal playing field. So it's up to you how you organise it, and what and how you make it look and feel. Be creative. You could stick in images and photographs, doodle, copy poems and passages from books and articles or write a favourite quote on the inside cover or first page. How about personalising the front cover? On days when nothing comes to her, poet Molly Gordon copies out passages from books by hand and novelist Janet Fitch always reads poetry before she writes, to sensitise her to the music and rhythm of language.

Play with your journal. Turn it upside down and write in different colours for different days of the week. Gillie Bolton is a reflective writing consultant and author of several books on the creative writing process. One person she worked with wrote, '*I like green ink: it is soothing and healing*' (2011). Bolton also suggests that children, along with health care and medical professionals, all love coloured paper and pens and that having these are a sign of respect. The sky's the limit. When keeping a journal or notebook feels more like play, it will pull you towards it rather than push you away. This is your journal initiation, the creative and original way you'll bring your notebook or journal alive.

The kind of notebook you choose is up to you. You may find it easier to have a notebook with lots of pages so you don't feel restricted and can spread yourself out. Or if that feels intimidating, maybe a small, pocket-sized notebook would work for you. You may prefer lined paper or an unlined notebook that gives you more freedom. Choose a notebook or journal that feels right for you.

Make sure you date your pages, so you can track your entries.

WAY 2 First things first

'The seeds of the day are best planted in the first hour.' **Dutch proverb**

I hope by now you have your notebook and that you're raring to go. But before you dive in, it's worth considering the time of day you'll dedicate to working through the 'Write now' writing practices. I'm a strong advocate of 'first things first', a management concept popularised by the late Steven Covey in his book, *The Seven Habits of Highly Effective People* (2004). The idea is that you place the most important task of your day at the top of your to do list and this becomes the first thing you do. Interestingly, there are writers who talk of feeling out of sorts when they miss writing for a day, something I notice I feel too.

You'll be encouraged to practise writing first thing in your day before you do any other tasks, as far as possible. This will be difficult for many of you, but not impossible. Even though you may be wondering how you'll find the time to make it happen, know that for many writers this is their normal practice and they make it work. So whether it means getting up 30 minutes earlier or setting off earlier so you can grab half an hour over a cup of tea in the café on your way to work, consider what might need to change to fit it into your schedule. Use your journal to make a list of ways you could fit your writing in as one of the first things you do in your day.

A second reason that many well-intentioned individuals fail to write and make space for writing is that they haven't given enough thought or consideration to what time of day

they'll schedule their time to write. Whether it's first thing in the morning or last thing at night, scheduling the time and place makes a big difference. It's so easy to zone out and believe that your good intentions will be enough to get you onto the page. Years of trial and error have convinced me that this is often not the case. Wishing doesn't amount to action and I'll show you why.

In his book, *Be Excellent at Anything*, Tony Schwartz (2011) introduces the concept of 'implementation intentions'. In one study carried out by Automaticity researchers (Gollwitzer & Brandstatter, 1997), a group of students was asked to write a report over the holidays describing what they'd done on Christmas Eve. Half the group identified specifically where and when they would write. The other half weren't given specific instructions about when or where to write. Only a third of the second group completed the task. However, more than three quarters of the first group completed the task. This was further reinforced in another study with chronic procrastinators carried out by psychology professor Peter Gollwitzer (1999). Chronic procrastinators who set a specific time to complete a task were eight times more likely to do so. It appears that when we work out the logistics we expend less energy thinking about the task and we get on and do it.

In another study, a group of subjects was asked to exercise for at least 20 minutes during the next week (Schwartz, 2011). Only 29 per cent of the group met the challenge. A second group was given the same challenge along with detailed information about the significant role exercise plays in reducing the risk of heart disease. Only 30 per cent met the challenge. A third group was invited to commit to exercising at a specific time, on a specific day, at a designated location. Engagement for this group more than doubled, to 91 per cent.

By knowing when and how you approach a task, you will reduce the amount of energy you'll expend on getting it done. I had this experience when I was a long distance runner. I would wake up every morning at the same time, 5am. I'd have my running clothes ready at the foot of my bed and my keys on the floor at the front door. I ran for almost 365 days every year for three years, in all weathers.

I ran even when I didn't feel like it – and I felt like that most mornings of the week. Running became an automatic habit and second nature.

SEE ALSO
- **WAY 3: Free writing** (page 26)
- **WAY 4: Morning pages** (page 28)
- **WAY 6: Writing habits and rituals** (page 32)
- **WAY 7: Writing prompts** (page 34)
- **WAY 8: Visual writing prompts** (page 39)

Making a commitment

As we have seen, it seems that being specific makes a difference to your level of commitment and engagement. So while we're hot on the subject, how about deciding on the following and writing them in your journal or notebook.

- Days of the week you will write
- Time of the day you will write
- Space your writing will take place in
- Date you made this commitment with yourself

Write now

Tip: You might want to consider how your energy levels vary throughout your day. When is your energy at its peak? When does your energy level slump? Notice the time of the day when you're most distracted. There does seem to be support for the effectiveness of writing first thing in the morning, before you do anything else in your day. However, if this doesn't work for you, then a better, more convenient time to write might be when your energy levels peak. Once you've identified when that is in your day, you can schedule this into your diary as your time in the day to write.

Business coach Charlie Gilkey has a really good downloadable tool on his website called a Productivity Heat Map (www.productiveflourishing.com/how-heatmapping-your-productivity-can-make-you-more-productive/) that will help you determine when those different energy states are during your day. You'll find the download details in Useful Resources on page 146.

WAY 3 Free writing

'A good way to start is to start badly.'
Robert Holden, 2012 (author and coach)

The roots of free writing (or free-fall writing as it is sometimes called) originated in the work of Sigmund Freud and Josef Breuer on free association*. Free association is a method of psychological analysis in which a person speaks or writes all the thoughts that come into their mind, whether the thoughts are related or not. It allows individuals to make connections consciously and retrieve repressed feelings without being judged.

Writer WO Mitchell further developed and introduced the free-fall method for creative writing. In his preface to *Free-Fall, An Anthology of the Writing Division*, Mitchell wrote that the method helped writers find their *'unlimited supply of: sensuous fragments, bits of people, dialogues, emotions and insights'* (Garner, 2009). He believed that his free-fall method, which he also called 'Mitchell's Messy Method', allowed writers to overcome their *'critical judgment'* and draw from their *'uncritical spontaneity'*.

There are many ways to empty the body – running, walking, gardening, boxing and any craft that uses the hands. Consider free writing as the mental process for emptying both the body and the mind. There is a freedom about free-fall or free writing. Many people freeze when it comes to a blank page. Free writing will help you to fill it. This technique gives you, the writer, permission to write without a destination or agenda. With free writing, you don't have to know what you're going to be writing about. Just go with the first thoughts that come into your mind and get it down on the page, then the next, and the one after that and so on. The rest will come.

At its core, free writing undoes the instinctive habit of editing and censoring your writing as you go along, a behaviour you may be familiar with and one that can unconsciously sabotage your attempts to get it onto the page when writing therapeutically. This domain is controlled by the voice of your inner critic*. You'll learn more about this in **WAY 9: Inner wise writing self** (page 40).

The inner critic* likes it when you go slowly, so it has the time to pick at your words, phrases and images – so write fast. Think of your inner critic* dozing off to sleep as you free write. Because of the lack of a destination and because you don't need to pay attention to grammar, your inner critic* can well be fooled into thinking that what you're doing is of very little substance. But this is a mistake. It's not that everything you free write will make great writing material but rather that this form of writing affords freedom for self-expression without any strings attached, and creates room for surprising and unexpected thoughts and discoveries to emerge. You may be surprised by the richness that is generated through regular practice and engagement with free writing.

Free writing practice

Remember there are no mistakes with free writing. How about starting now with your first free writing practice? Turn to a blank page in your notebook and free write for 20 minutes. Start with the very first thought that comes into your head. When you've finished, take three deep breaths, close your notebook, stretch. Take a couple of minutes away from your writing space and go for a short walk. In **WAY 7: Writing prompts** (page 34) you'll find a collection of prompts that will help you with free writing when you get stuck or don't know what to say.

Write now

Tristine Rainer (1978) says in *The New Diary*, 'Write fast, write everything, include everything, write from your feelings, write from your body, accept whatever comes'. The guidelines for free writing are simple:

- You can write about anything.
- Write as fast as you can.
- Write for no more than 20 minutes.
- Writing by hand is the preferred method.
- Don't worry about grammar or spelling.
- It doesn't have to make sense.
- If you get stuck, write what's in your head.
- There's no need to edit or censor, just get it all down on the page.

SEE ALSO
- **WAY 2: First things first** (page 24)
- **WAY 4: Morning pages** (page 28)
- **WAY 6: Writing habits and rituals** (page 32)
- **WAY 7: Writing prompts** (page 34)
- **WAY 8: Visual writing prompts** (page 39)

Tip: Free-fall writing is a writing technique that will warm you up so that you don't arrive cold to the 'Write now' exercises. Try free writing for 20 minutes before you start these. You can also use the free-writing method to keep on writing throughout your day. This is a refreshing and cathartic method for emptying the mind as much as possible in advance of starting other writing practices.

4 Morning pages

'Every time you write, something valuable will occur.' SARK, 2012 (author)

Morning pages* are a version of free writing but with a twist. The technique originated from the work of writer Julia Cameron and was introduced in her best selling book *The Artist's Way* (1982).

Having done work in recovery and the 12 Steps programme, Cameron uses the morning pages* technique to help her maintain and sustain her own recovery. She attributes her daily practice of writing morning pages* as the real champion of her inner work. Morning pages*, like free writing, is stream of consciousness writing but with specifics built in.

- First, you write first thing in the morning. This is one of the cornerstones of the morning pages* writing practice, the idea being that your thoughts are in their most natural and pure state first thing in the morning, and you're more likely to capture these raw and uncensored thoughts when you write as soon as you awake.

- Second, you write a stream of consciousness by hand only, a point Cameron has stuck to over 25 years of teaching her fundamental creativity practices.

- Third, you write three pages only and go no further (although, of course, you don't castigate yourself if you do more).

- Fourth, you write as fast as you can. That way, your inner editor won't be able to keep up with your pace. In one of her books, Cameron describes the editor as moving at 35 miles per hour; when you write fast, you are writing at around 70 miles per hour. I like the idea of speeding past your editor.

At first glance, what you produce might feel like a moaning shop – and it might well be that way. But have faith because over time you'll notice subtle and sometimes substantial shifts in your writing. Danny Gregory, author of *The Creative License* (2006), sees many potentials in the use of his journals, including shifting from a place of catharsis to one of contemplation. He suggests that the journal should not be a dumping ground but a place to create, recognise and celebrate. Even so, your moans and groans are now out of your head and safely contained on the page, making space for your creative brain to take over. Cameron advocates that morning pages* give you the space to dump those toxic thoughts and create room for the more creative and imaginative thoughts that are often lurking beneath the surface. It's a writing practice that unclutters the mind.

By writing as fast as you can, without censoring or editing what you write, Cameron believes you write straight past your inner critic*, shape-shifting past its determined efforts to put the brakes on your writing and creative pursuits.

You can read more about morning pages* in one of Cameron's many books on writing, creativity and spirituality. My favourites are listed in the Useful Resources section on page 146.

First thing tomorrow

Tomorrow morning, before you even get out of bed, turn to a blank page in your journal or notebook, date the page and write three pages in longhand as fast as you can, capturing whatever thoughts are in your head or whatever you are thinking or feeling. If you come to a blank, simply write, 'I don't know what to write' and follow this up with whatever comes next.

Some of the benefits you'll gain from free writing and morning pages* practices include:

- engagement in a mindful practice that brings your awareness and attention into the here and now
- a non-traditional form of meditation that may be more suitable for your way of learning
- a helpful way to solve problems and find solutions
- a useful mirror to reveal both strengths and weaknesses
- a gateway for suppressed emotions and feelings to be released
- access to the sixth sense of intuition* (sometimes referred to as your inner-tuition) through the discoveries, and often recovery, made through the practice of writing morning pages*
- strengthening the core of your inner wise writing self*
- deepening your resilience as you cultivate a resource that will strengthen your inner being
- you're more likely to consider impulses or random ideas that are easily dismissed at other times of the day.

SEE ALSO

- **WAY 3: Free writing** (page 26)
- **WAY 6: Writing habits and rituals** (page 32)
- **WAY 7: Writing prompts** (page 34)
- **WAY 8: Visual writing prompts** (page 39)
- **WAY 23: A paper ritual for releasing your emotions** (page 76)
- **WAY 48: A letter to you** (page 138)

> **Tip:** Writing morning pages* is a good way of waking up to yourself on the page and performing a writing dump before you approach one of the 'Write now' exercises. Writing by hand slows you down and allows you the time and space to connect with yourself on a deeper level.

Writing spaces

'We all need to have a creative outlet – a window, a space – so we don't lose track of ourselves.' **Norman Fischer, 2001 (poet and Zen teacher)**

By now you will have decided what time of the day you will write. We're now going to talk about writing stations – the spaces you inhabit to write in or from. Creating routines around your writing can be helpful, but there will also be value in changing the spaces in which you write, when you want to shift or gain new perspectives on your writing.

With just a notebook and pen or pencil to hand, almost anywhere is a potential writing station. I can think of two places in which it would be hard to write – in a police cell and in water – but I'm sure, with a bit of imagination, you could find ways to write perfectly well in both of those contexts. You could write on your body, for example, or, as in the music of singer and songwriter Rachel Fuller, who hates writing on paper, you could write on walls. She likes the permanence of this medium and the fact that you have to think carefully before you commit yourself. Members of the public often write on the walls of public spaces and we call it graffiti. It's definitely worth considering which space works best for you. But first, let's take a moment to review some of the spaces and ways in which writers past and present have written.

- Anne Dilliard likes a room with no view and Maya Angelou writes in hotel rooms with no windows.

- Danyel Smith engaged in a writing marathon on a three-day cross country train journey. His train journey became a writing retreat; filling journals, words became sentences, became chapters and eventually became novels.

- SARK, Colette, James Joyce and Edith Wharton all enjoyed the comforts of writing in bed.

- Alan Greenspan, the former chairman of the US Federal Reserve, wrote 85 per cent of his most recent book in the bathtub.

- Sam Shepard writes on highways and Gertrude Stein composed poems at the wheel of her parked car.

- Benjamin Zephaniah once frequented a bench in the middle of a roundabout in Stratford when he needed to create a space where he could think.

Consider what might be essential for you in your writing space, both physically and psychologically. Do you need comfort? Is lighting important? Do you need to be sitting or standing? Like Anne Dilliard and Maya Angelou, do you need to a room without a view to avoid distraction? Are you disturbed by sound or will background noise actually relax you? Does it need to be warm? Do you prefer inside or outside? Make a list of the essentials that you require for an ideal writing station.

SEE ALSO
- **WAY 6: Writing habits and rituals** (page 32)
- **WAY 7: Writing prompts** (page 34)
- **WAY 10: Stilling the mind to write** (page 42)
- **WAY 40: Writing with nature** (page 118)
- **WAY 42: Walking and writing** (page 126)

'Write any place'

Find a comfy seat or somewhere to sit outside with your notebook and pen for half an hour. Work through as many of the prompts below as you can, writing down your responses and thinking in your notebook. When you have finished, read over what you have written and draw up a plan for your writing spaces on different days of the week. Give yourself different places to write on different days of the week – in your car, leaning against a tree or on the top of a double decker bus. Nowhere is off limits for your notebook, pen and you. Natalie Goldberg (1986) reminds us, *'when we are in the heart of writing it doesn't matter where we are: it is perfect. There is a great sense of autonomy and security to know we can write any place.'*

Write now

Here are some ideas of writing stations you could choose from:

At home
- Your bed
- Your desk
- The kitchen or dining room table
- A comfy chair or sofa
- A quiet spot on a hallway or staircase
- Your garden
- In the bath
- A closet or small cupboard

At work
- Your desk
- Meeting room
- Outside area
- Staff canteen
- At your computer with headphones on

Outside
- Cafés
- Museums and galleries
- Hotel lobbies and foyers
- Libraries
- Restaurants, pubs and bars
- Parks and green spaces
- Sitting with your back against a tree
- Public transport, buses, trains and planes
- Your car
- A bench in a busy shopping mall

Use these writing prompts to explore further thoughts and reflections about other possible writing spaces:

- What other writing spaces can you think of?
- What are your three favourite writing spots?
- What is it you like about these spaces?
- What two new spaces might you have a go at writing in?
- What's your least favourite writing spot? Make a point of visiting this space to write in it at least once.
- What days of the week are you most likely to write in your three favourite writing spaces, and how often?
- Where else might you consider a possible writing spot?
- Bring in the senses. What smells would stimulate your writing juices? What textures would you enjoy having around you? What visual scenes would be pleasing to the eye? What sounds would you find soothing?
- What are the silent spaces in your neighbourhood where you can go and write?

WAY 6

Writing habits and rituals

'Rituals help us to do just that. They give us a structure, the basic scaffold that invites us to take time away from our busy days in the hope of bringing mindfulness to our emotional lives.' Deborah Globus, e-book (LaPadre – a non-denominational minister)

What would it take to entice you to your journal or writing notebook on a regular basis? I know a warm space usually coaxes me to the page, or having a notebook by my bed. Performing an action, such as lighting a candle or incense stick, sends me a message that I'm setting my intention to write, and the ritual of lighting the candle is my marker, my gateway that I'm about to start. In many ways, a ritual is you setting the intention by saying to yourself that you're moving into that sacred space, that meditative mindset that declares you're preparing to write. You can consciously invoke rituals or special things that you do that will stimulate your interest in getting out your notebook or journal to write. No matter how strong you believe your willpower is, it won't get you to the page. So having rituals in place can be a key part of your success.

For years, I've collected index cards on which I've meticulously copied examples of the writing rituals of writers from different genres. Isabel Allende starts all her books on 8 January each year, while Wayne Dyer and Anthony Burgess all share the same ritual of starting a new book or new journal on 1 January of each year. Strange as it may sound, the poet Friedrich Schiller used to keep rotten apples under the lid of his desk and inhale their pungent bouquet when he needed to find the right word. Researchers at Yale University have since discovered that the smell of spiced apples has a powerful elevating effect on people and can even stave off panic attacks (Brandeis, 2002).

Your ritual doesn't need to be as elaborate or strange as this; in fact, the simpler the better. What anchors the ritual in place is that it's pleasurable and repetitive. For example, you could get up at the same time each morning and write, and then reward yourself with a cup of coffee or tea. Like writing stations in **WAY 5: Writing spaces** (page 30), you may need a range of rituals to maintain momentum so you won't get bored. So, at home, your ritual might be making a steaming cup of coffee and sitting in your favourite chair. At work, it might be using a coloured pen that is distinctly different from the black or blue ink you use for your work. Your ritual can be as personal and as obvious as you like. It is your calling card to the page, so make it work for you.

Don't forget to schedule in when your ritual will happen, as well. In his book, *Be Excellent at Anything: Four changes to get more out of work and life*, Tony Schwartz (2011) writes, *'By defining precisely when we're going to undertake a behaviour, we reduce the amount of energy we have to expend to get it done'*.

Creating ritual

- Make a list of rituals you can create that will pull you towards your writing. Make them things you will look forward to, that are easy to do or that have enjoyment or benefit for you.

- What will you do before you write? You could perform the alternate nostril breathing technique introduced in **WAY 10: Stilling the mind to write** (page 42). How about playing a piece of music? Will smelling a certain fragrance or scent entice you to the page? Will the luxury of writing on nice paper do the trick?

- Would scheduling different spaces in which to write energise you and keep you engaged?

- Planning your rituals in advance could make all the difference.

Do whatever it takes to launch your spirit and soul into writing mode.

Write now

Psychologists refer to a concept called Hebbs Law*, which states that 'neurons that fire together stay together'. This connects to the neuroscience* concept of neuroplasticity*. By ritualising your writing, you can create pleasant experiences that are then laid over positive associations for writing. This creates new neural pathways that challenge any fears and anxieties you may have around negative experiences of writing.

The act of simple ritual calms nerves and unwires previous held negative neural pathways. Research into the neuroscience* of the brain has recognised that the brain is not hard wired, as was previously thought, but in fact the brain has huge potential to change based on your actions and choices (Bane, 2012). In time, your rituals will bring about the state of mind that pulls you into your writing.

SEE ALSO
- **WAY 5: Writing spaces** (page 30)
- **WAY 10: Stilling the mind to write** (page 42)
- **WAY 40: Writing with nature** (page 118)
- **WAY 41: Conversations with trees** (page 122)
- **WAY 42: Walking and writing** (page 126)

WAY 7 Writing prompts

'A writer travels wherever their pen takes them: alone, nearly in silence, and for themselves. Not knowing where, and what they want to bring back, is vital, just as Alice found with her explorations in Wonderland.' Gillie Bolton, 2011 (consultant in reflective writing)

Writing prompts are sometimes just one word, sentence or quote that gives you a nudge to get writing across the blank page. They're graceful and creative writing tools, useful on those days when you feel stuck, you don't know what to write about or you're just not in the mood for writing. Judy Reeves, author of *A Writer's Book of Days* (1999), has some of the best writing prompts around and describes writing prompts as *'music that invites you to dance'*.

Writing prompts are one of the best ways I know of helping you get unblocked and past any fears you might have about how to start and continue writing when you're not sure what you want to say. With this kind of writing there's no need to start off knowing what you're going to write.

The more you write, the more you'll move towards what it is you want to say. Prompts are great tools to combine with your free writing or morning pages* practices.

Hold the writing prompt lightly, and don't forget to use it to free associate with whatever comes to mind. Remember, there's no one looking over your shoulder and you're not being graded. The prompt is not intended to be written in stone but is rather a springboard onto the blank page. Once you have those first few words down, even if they don't relate to the prompt, you're then free to go wherever you want with your writing. That's the real beauty of a writing prompt: you can write about something totally unrelated or disconnected from it. The prompt will have achieved its goal of getting you going.

Here is a list of ideas for writing prompts that you can use in your writing practice:

- I remember
- Fondest memory of childhood
- Best friend growing up
- First day at school
- First job
- First boyfriend or girlfriend
- First room of my own
- First car
- First trip abroad
- First night alone
- It took me by surprise
- It was a full moon
- The buses and train had all stopped

SEE ALSO
- **WAY 8: Visual writing prompts** (page 39)
- **WAY 32: Question time** (page 96)

Making your own prompts

How about making your own set of writing prompts? You'll need a few sheets of coloured paper or card (packets of luggage tags also make great writing prompts) cut into strips.

To get started, you could print the bullets opposite or the writing and inner knowing writing prompts box sets on pages 36 and 37, or write them out by hand. Store your slips in an envelope (making them easy to carry around with you) or a small tin or box, and keep them in one of your writing locations.

When you feel stuck or are not sure what to say, pick a random writing prompt and free write for 20 minutes.

Over time, build up your collection of writing prompts by cutting out articles and story headlines from magazines or newspapers, or collecting lines from articles and books. Song titles can make great writing prompts.

Make collecting writing prompts an ongoing project and create them from whatever comes to your attention.

Having your notebook to hand will be very useful.

Write now

Writing prompts box set

If my life had no limits, what would I be doing?	Describe your hands	What do I not want to write or talk about today?	Pause in the middle of your day and answer the question, 'How is my day going?'
Noise	**Unravelling**	**Doorway**	**Breathing**
What I want to write about today	Start your free writing by writing about the weather	The full moon in the sky	What would happen if you could?
A strong memory from my childhood	The time when I forgot	I really, really, really want	This is the thing I'm least proud of...
Silence	**Healing**	**Hunger**	**Unbelonging**
Eyes closed shut	What's most uncomfortable right now for me?	A tree I remember	What I'm not writing about
Roots	**Lost**	**Holding**	**Fallen**
Then the rain came	I'm not sure	If I were an animal I'd be...	Describe five things about the person you last spoke with
Flight	**Topaz**	**Spirit**	**Honey bees**
Describe one of the homes you've lived in to a complete stranger	A childhood taste	Write about your school days	Write about a friend from the past
Intuition	**Shadows**	**Treasure box**	**Mangoes**
Write about the building or place you're sitting in	Write about the last meal you ate	Write a letter to someone you admire	Write a letter to your inner wise writing self
Surrender	**Uncertainty**	**Awe**	**Delight**
Last night I had a dream	The sky had no stars in the sky	It was a hot, humid night	A memory of holding someone's hand
Music	**Dancing**	**Forget-me-nots**	**Warm**

Inner knowing writing prompts box set

How are you better off than you were three years ago?	What has surprised you most about how your life has turned out?	What's something you've appreciated since you've grown older?	When you look in the mirror, who do you see?
What, other than food, are you hungry for?	What opportunity did you let slip through your fingers?	What are five ways you could add more fun to your life?	What do you do when you feel like giving up?
If you left your life tomorrow, how would people remember you?	When was the last time you lost track of doing something you really enjoyed?	What do you wish you'd done differently?	In the busy-ness of your daily life, what are you not seeing?
What are ten things other people do not know about you?	What would you do if you knew you couldn't fail?	What three things do you need in your life to be happy?	What's missing from your life?
What's the biggest disappointment of your life so far?	What's your most powerful life memory that involves you?	What could you make more time to do every day?	What habit is standing between you and what you want?
If you had to save only seven items from a house fire, what items would you save?	If you had the chance to go back in life and change one thing, what would it be?	What will you never tell?	What are three areas of help/support you could do with in your life right now?
What is your most cherished childhood memory?	What was your life like this time ten years ago?	What are five small, simple things that give you joy?	What stands between you and your full potential?
What's the scariest thing you've ever done?	What are you sure of?	What are you unsure of?	What are ten things you'd love to have a go at?

WAY 8

Visual writing prompts

'It is looking at things for a long time that ripens you and gives you a deeper understanding' Vincent Van Gogh (painter) (Gregory, 2006)

Visual writing prompts can be used in the same way as writing prompts. They say a picture paints a thousand words. Sometimes an image will sink deeper into the unconscious process and reveal more than words could say about your feelings and emotions at the time. Pictures and images can help you find the language of your soul and spirit when words cannot communicate the language of what you're feeling.

Start by leafing through magazines and tearing out images that speak to you. At the same time, be on the lookout for strong and provocative words and headlines that can also serve as writing prompts.

Collect postcards and images as you go about your day-to-day life and add these to the pool.

Images and photos tell a story, but you can be the narrator of what the image means to you. Here are some suggestions you can use to explore your visual writing prompts:

- Write about how the image makes you feel.
- What do you really see?
- How are you like, or not like, the image?
- What's missing from this image?
- What's a new narrative for your image?
- Think of a problem or challenge you're having. Select a random image to gain insight or new perspectives on the issue. How does this image relate to the problem or issue you're having?
- Close your eyes and choose an image.

Have fun. There are so many ways to learn about yourself.

SEE ALSO
- **WAY 7: Writing prompts** (page 34)
- **WAY 32: Question time** (page 96)

Inner wise writing self

'You could search the whole world over and never find anyone as deserving of your love as yourself.' **Buddha**

A major part of your journey to write yourself well will be to deepen your connection to your inner wise writing self*. Creativity expert and writer SARK is the creator of the concept of the inner wise self, a well-known spiritual principle. It's that part of the self that affirms your wholeness; the part that nurtures and nourishes who you are. In her many books and e-courses, SARK suggests writing letters to and from the inner wise self on a regular basis, a practice I would like you to adopt. We'll refer to it here as your inner wise writing self*.

Take a moment and close your eyes. Imagine a part of you that knows and understands the many healing and therapeutic benefits of writing. The inner wise writing self* is a sacred and holy part of you that loves, supports and nourishes your writing and creative self. Your inner wise writing self* knows what possibilities are waiting to unfold onto the page. Once you give yourself permission to write and you regularly show up, the inner wise writing self* will guide you to all those places waiting to be tapped into. Everyone has an inner writer – a part of the self that is deeply connected to the treasure trove of words, stories and memories that are yours to bestow on the page.

Writing regularly to and from your inner wise writing self* is a perfect method for strengthening this part of yourself to support and nourish your writing practice. You can write regularly, when you feel unsure or disheartened, when you're stuck about what to write or when you've just connected with a painful or difficult memory. Let him or her know that you have lost your way, that you're unsure and that you need reminding, and ask for guidance back to the page. Remember that the voice of the inner wise writing self* is affirming. It knows the truth of who you are and will always find the right words to get you back on track.

Here's a short excerpt from one of my own letters from my inner wise writing self* during the writing of this book:

Dearest Darling Jackee,

I'm really enjoying meeting with you every day. I can feel how deep you're sinking into moulding and shaping this book, and the boundless learning and connections it is generating for you. I am seeing your confidence and your creativity rise as you have enjoyed the seamless moments of flow the writing process has opened to you. I love the fact that you're smiling more from the inside and that you look forward to being with your writing self. I look forward to enjoying more of your company over the coming weeks and months. I'm sure you'll be digging deeper and revealing more of the wonders that writing has to offer you.

Don't forget to look after your body and to continue to invest in your self-care. Your body is the vehicle through which we communicate. It is the holder of your stories and your experiences, and is what keeps you present. Nurture her as well. Without the body, there would be no writer.

With love, Your Inner Wise Writing Self xxxxxxx

Accessing your inner wise writing self

Carve out some space in your day where you can sit down undisturbed with a cup of tea.

Write your first letter to yourself from your inner wise writing self*. Invite your inner wise writing self* to affirm all your qualities that make it worthwhile for you to show up on the page. Your inner wise writing self* knows the part of you that dreams and is visionary. It has an eye for the parts of you that are good, talented, glorious, wild and original. All the wonderful things that make you who you are.

It's the part of you that knows you can write, knows what you need to express on the page and is not afraid to dive beneath the surface and emerge with the words and stories in service of your healing and transformation. Even if you don't feel like writing your first letter, do it and see what comes. When you've finished writing your letter, put your notebook down and go and do something nourishing for yourself. You'll be receiving letters from your inner wise writing self* throughout this journey.

Write now

Other creative ways of working with your inner wise writing self* are:

- Posing daily questions. What do I need to remember today? What's the most important thing for me to be writing about today?
- Using your non-dominant hand* to write to your inner wise writing self*. There is more on the benefits of this in **WAY 13: Writing with your non-dominant hand** (page 50).
- Using rituals to create a sacred energy to coax your inner wise writing self* onto the page.

Your inner wise writing self* is a perfect deterrent to the voice of the inner critic*. For people who have expressed a desire to write for therapeutic purposes, the voice of their inner critic* can sometimes rob them of their ability to express themselves on the page. This book presupposes that you'll gain momentum and value from a regular writing practice. By doing so, you will notice over time the gradual decline of the volume of your inner critic's* voice.

> **Tip:** While the chapters on managing your emotions explore the concept of negative beliefs, there is no chapter in the book focusing on the inner critic*. Why? Because the inner critic* already gets too much of your time and attention. By investing time in regular communication with your inner wise writing self*, you'll strengthen the quality of this life-affirming part of who you are.

SEE ALSO
- **WAY 7: Writing prompts** (page 34)
- **WAY 13: Writing with your non-dominant hand** (page 50)
- **WAY 15: Writing the labyrinth** (page 54)
- **WAY 16: Finger walking the labyrinth** (page 58)

Stilling the mind to write

'Within you there is a stillness and a sanctuary to which you can retreat at any time.' Hermann Hesse, 1999 (novelist)

REVITALISING BREATHING PRACTICE

Writing is physical work and what you write about is deeply connected to your body and your breath. By becoming conscious of your body and your breath, you'll give licence to more of your stories to make it to the surface of the page and beyond.

In her wonderful book, *Writing Begins With The Breath*, Laraine Herring (2007) writes, *'Observing our breath gives us, as writers, an opportunity to truly embody the writing process in our cells'*. The breath is the bridge between the body and the page. It's a way of stilling the mind and mining the body for the depth of your experiences and stories.

It is in stillness that you will hear your own thoughts. Deep connective breathing will take you into the core of your being and return what you find there to the page.

Try this simple kundalini yoga breathing practice, called the Nadi Shodhana alternate nostril breathing exercise. It is a simple practice you can implement at the start or finish of any of the writing practices suggested in this book. This practice is also ideal when you need to calm down, when your mind is racing fast or when you can't go to sleep.

- Block off your right nostril by putting gentle pressure on it with your right thumb.

- Taking a long, slow, deep breath, gently inhale through your left nostril. Then, just as gently, exhale slowly and completely, again through the left nostril.

- Do the same again, this time blocking your left nostril and breathing through your right nostril.

- Relax your body as you feel the cooling breath flowing through your body. Relax even deeper with each exhale, as you breathe out all the tension, stress and toxins in your body. As you become more practised with your breathing practice, try inhaling for four counts, holding for four and exhaling for four.

Benefits of this breathing practice include:
- It increases mental clarity and a deep, full relaxation or even sleep.
- It brings balance to the left and right hemispheres of the mind.
- If you inhale through the right nostril and exhale through the left, it helps to make you calm, while integrating unwanted negative emotions and stress.
- If you inhale through the left nostril and exhale through the right, it gives clarity and promotes positive mood. It also helps you focus on what's important.
- If you make the inhaled breath longer than the exhaled breath, you stimulate the sympathetic part of the autonomic nervous system, boost the heart rate and blood pressure, boost alertness and stimulate the nervous system.

- If you emphasise the exhaled breath, you stimulate the parasympathetic nervous system, slow down the heartbeat and relax the circulation, nerves and digestive systems.
- You're feeding your body with oxygen, which will energise you.

There's one more point I want to make on stilling the mind before, during and after you write. I have read this summarised no better than Eric Maisel in his book *Deep Writing: 7 Principles that bring ideas to life* (1999). He suggests eliminating the demons that ward you off from the page, just by 'hushing'. Maisel writes, '...*and often I do say, "Hush. Hush. Write a little." My goal is to quiet the nerves and minds of the participants, to let the anxiety be normalised, embraced, dissipated, to silence the demons by naming them and then smiling... All I do is provide a path to right silence.*'

A REMINDER OF WHAT YOU NEED

Finally, here's a reminder of what you need to prepare yourself to write. Perhaps there will be days when you won't have all the suggestions in place and indeed you won't need all of them, all of the time. But doing these practices will both strengthen and nourish your writing and make it a richer learning experience, both on and off the page.

- Have your writing kit ready to hand: notebook or journal, paper, pen or pencil and a rubber for your drawings.
- Decide on the space you'll be writing in.
- Enter into an alternate nostril breathing practice for three minutes (see opposite).
- Perform your opening ritual.
- Begin your chosen practice method: free writing, morning pages*, 'Write now' practice or visual or writing prompt.

- When you've finished writing or you get stuck, get up and move to break your state. Put your papers down and take a quick walk or stretch. This is not just physical work, it's emotional and mental work too, and looking after yourself is essential to maintaining your health and well-being. If you feel you need a longer time away from your writing, by all means give yourself permission to do so. Go off and do something entirely different and return when you're ready. Make sure that on your return and before you start, you take four long deep breaths or do the Nadi Shodhana breathing practice again.
- Remember to drink lots of water as you write.
- Build in small treats and rewards.

SEE ALSO
- **WAY 15: Writing the labyrinth** (page 54)
- **WAY 16: Finger-walking the labyrinth** (page 58)

1 2 3 4 5 6 7 8
9 10 **11 12 13 14**
15 16 17 18 19
20 21 22 23 24
25 26 27 28 29
30 31 32 33 34
35 36 37 38 39
40 41 42 43 44
45 46 47 48 49

Chapter 2

ESCAPE THE DIGITAL: WHY WRITING BY HAND WITH PEN AND PAPER WORKS

This chapter looks at why writing by hand makes a difference and explores creative ways of engaging with your journals and notebooks. The digital world is rapidly taking the place of the ancient tradition of writing by hand. This chapter outlines some of the benefits of writing by hand and how it differs from writing with a keyboard and computer. You will discover the benefits of writing with your non-dominant hand* and how to use it to gain and mine your own inner wisdom. By connecting with the messages and language of your non-dominant hand* you can try out the 'Write now' practice of identifying your inner animal by using both the dominant and non-dominant hands*. You will have fun drawing and discover how drawing in your journals and notebooks can improve your observational abilities and allow you to sit more in the present moment. You will learn how drawing or using images can capture the language that words on a page sometimes miss. You can also practise taking a problem or challenge on a writing walk on the page through the sacred ritual of 'walking the labyrinth'.

WAY 11

Why write by hand?

'Of all the ways we express ourselves non-verbally, none is quite so personal as our handwriting... Unlike other ways we express our individuality, we have sole ownership of our handwriting.'
Betty Edwards, 2008 (art therapist)

With handwriting fast becoming a lost art, which do you think is better – writing by hand or using a keyboard? This is a subject of debate among many writers and there are, of course, advantages and disadvantages to both approaches.

In the course of writing yourself well, I would suggest that as far as possible you attempt as many of the writing practices by hand as possible, particularly the morning pages* and free writing practices. There are a number of reasons for this and many are supported by research and feedback from writers.

Writing by hand keeps the practice of writing deeply connected to the body. Your body is an accurate messenger and receptacle for your vast range of feelings and emotions. Writing by hand is the most natural way for you to stay connected and plugged into your body's extensive data system.

Writing by hand has a stronger sensual connection. The feel of your skin touching the pen or pencil it holds, the texture of the pen or pencil nib against the paper's surface, the pressure of your writing on the page, all provide a more sensory experience than pressing the letters on a keyboard.

In a recent study led by Karin Harman James, assistant professor of psychology and neuroscience at Indiana State University, reported in the *Journal of Cognitive Neuroscience*, adults were first asked to produce new characters using either a pen and paper or a computer keyboard. They were then asked to distinguish between the new characters and mirror images of them. Those writing by hand retained stronger and lasting recognition of the characters' proper orientation.

Virginia Berninger, Professor of Educational Psychology at the University of Washington, says that handwriting differs from typing because it requires sequential strokes to form letters whereas keyboarding involves selecting a letter by touching a key (Bounds, 2010). Sequential finger movement activates massive regions involved in thinking, language and working memory.

Writing by hand is an act of mindfulness*. Many writers report that when they write using a keyboard they tend to write much faster than when they write by hand. The question then is: how mindful are we when we type as opposed to write? Even when you write quickly using pen and paper, notice how writing by hand slows you down, has more space for pauses, space to connect and, most importantly, space to breathe. This slower pace allows you become more present and mindful in the moment.

Writers have a bit to say on the topic of writing by hand. Amy Tan composes her final drafts on a computer but handwrites everything during the note-taking stage of a book. Paul Auster sticks with his fountain pen and paper but then types out a page on an old manual typewriter at the end of the day. Anne Tyler writes with a Parker 75 Fountain pen using a no 62 nib filled with black ink on unlined paper.

Your most beautiful 'hand'

- Choose a random page from this book and copy half of the text on the page using your most beautiful 'hand' – your best handwriting.

- Now copy out the same page using your non-dominant writing hand. Take your time and notice what it feels like to write using your non-dominant hand*. There is more on this in **WAY 13: Writing with your non-dominant hand** (page 50).

- Copy out the same page using a computer keyboard.

- Return to your dominant writing hand and free write about what it was like using the three different approaches. What did you notice and feel? What different things did you pick up from the three approaches? Try to identify what was different about each approach.

Write now

Betty Edwards has a wonderful chapter on handwriting in *The New Drawing on the Right Side of the Brain* (2008) in which she questions whether we can regain this lost art. She points out that, *'...handwriting can function as a means of artistic expression'*. Edwards believes that your signature expresses you, your individuality and your creativity.

Research by Virginia Berninger (Bounds 2010) has found that different parts of the brain are triggered when writing at a computer versus writing with pen or pencil, proving that we think and feel differently when we write by hand than when we use a computer. Writing by hand is also linked to firing up the neurons required for creative thinking to a much greater degree than when we write using a keyboard.

An experiment carried out by Dr Lieberman, psychologist at the University of California (Sample 2009), found that writing about feelings and penning poetry helped regulate emotions. Volunteers were invited to a brain

scan then asked to write for 20 minutes a day for four consecutive days. Half the group wrote about a recent emotional experience and the other half wrote about a neutral experience. Those writing about an emotional experience had more activity in a key part of the brain that reduced neural activity connected to strong emotional feelings. It was found that writing by hand had a bigger impact than typing and that men seemed to benefit from writing about their feelings more than women.

In general, then, research is indicating that there are significant benefits to writing by hand and that it helps people deal with emotional distress.

SEE ALSO
- **WAY 12: Write it down to make it happen** (page 48)
- **WAY 13: Writing with your non-dominant hand** (page 50)

12

Write it down to make it happen

'The concept of neuroplasticity, the idea that the brain can change far more than we ever thought possible, is probably one of the landmark shifts in science.'
Roseanne Bane, 2012 (writing teacher and creativity coach)

WHAT'S THE SECRET TO WRITING DOWN YOUR GOALS?

Neuroscience* is finally confirming what the world of personal development has known for years – that there is a way of writing down your goals to ensure they're realised. When you write something down on a list or in a letter, you subconsciously activate emotions and energies that affect you in a specific way. This is supported by research such as that reported by Davis (2012).

Here are two stories from Henriette Anne Klauser's (2001) book, *Write It Down, Make It Happen*, that illustrate how writing down what you want and *acting as if it has been realised* can positively work for you once you have adopted a particular mindset.

The first account concerns Gloria, who wrote a letter to an imagined future partner almost daily for more than a year, even though she had no idea whether she would accomplish her goal. Writing the letters helped Gloria to feel how real a relationship could be. Over time, Gloria's desire to attract a partner was no longer driven by neediness or desperation because in each letter she also worked on her own fears and anxieties. By voicing her fears, she put distance between herself and her concerns. Writing became a way to vent and move on.

The second story involves Alice, who created a list detailing 100 qualities she was looking for in a partner. The list remained in Alice's closet for five years while she, too, got on with her life. When she did eventually meet her partner, much to her surprise many of the desired qualities on her list were present in the man she'd attracted. She had the proof on paper.

Your list has greater impact if you write it by hand than by using a computer. By articulating your desires on paper, you send out a strong message and intention to a part of your brain called the reticular activating system*. Imagine that the reticular activating system* is a massive search engine in your mind, which processes the data you send through it. So if you write down the specific qualities you're looking for in a partner or a job, for example, the reticular activating system* then gets to work, finding the evidence that will bring you what you want and filtering out anything that doesn't meet your requirements. So the more specific you are on paper, the easier it will be for the reticular activating system* to do its job.

The other thing that makes a difference is letting go of how your goal will be realised. This means developing a form of non-attachment to how the results are achieved or the length of time in which it happens. Think about the stories of Gloria and Alice: how might the reticular activating system* have impacted on the outcomes?

THE 'ACT AS IF' THEORY

Both Alice and Gloria may have been unconsciously acting on what is known as the 'act as if' theory developed by the psychologist William James. This theory is widely advocated in self-help circles, but less well known is its origin, which was in a lecture James gave in 1896, entitled *The Will To Believe*. The theory is based on the principle of adopting beliefs

The power of lists and letters

Decide when you'll have some time and space to yourself. Grab a cup of coffee or tea and find yourself a warm, cosy spot. Perform the alternate nostril breathing practice from **WAY 10: Stilling the mind to write** (page 42) before you start.

Choose one or more activities from the following list:

- Write a list or letter to yourself sharing 10 things you really believe about yourself – even if you don't.
- Write a list or letter to yourself describing 10 things you're looking for in a new partner. Aim to embody all those qualities in yourself first. Make a note of how many of those qualities you already possess.
- Write a list or letter of 20 things you want in a new job, home, business or any other goals or desires.
- Write a detailed description of what you really, really, really want. Explore the question again and again in your journal or notebook. This is called an inquiry question. Let your writing take you into deeper levels of inquiry about the question.

- Practise challenging 'functional fixedness'. This is a psychological concept that refers to seeing only one common use for an object and not being able to see outside of this. To challenge the notion of functional fixedness*, quick-think 10 ways you could ensure you believe in yourself, 10 ways you could meet your ideal mate, 10 ways you could go about attracting a new job...

You'll lend your lists and letters more weight by putting them on paper in your own handwriting. Be specific in your list-making or letter-writing, and date everything you create.

Once you've written your lists or letters, put them in a personal, sacred space like your journal, a photo album or the drawer of a bedside table. You could tear the pages from your notebook and mail them to yourself. Whatever you do with them, then leave them. Return to them in six months or even a year's time. Compare what has manifested from your list in your life. Capture your evidence in writing. What has been an even better outcome? What has surprised you?

Write now

without having the evidence. In other words, even if you have little evidence to support the possibility of reaching your goal or achieving your desired outcome, if you act as if it's possible, then something begins to shift.

Both Gloria and Alice used the power of writing to visualise, to bring into form their actual dreams and desires about specific life goals. They acted as if their goals were going to be

achieved without needing to know specifically how or when this would happen.

SEE ALSO
- **WAY 11: Why write by hand?** (page 46)
- **WAY 13: Writing with your non-dominant hand** (page 50)
- **WAY 24: Intuition – your inner wisdom** (page 78)

WAY 13 Writing with your non-dominant hand

'The non-dominant hand in a right-handed person – the left hand – is much more creative and less apt to be governed by the should and the shouldn't of the left brain, right hand.'
Bernard Selling, 2003 (author)

Which hand do you use to write with on a daily basis? Left or right? Let's focus on the hand you don't use. This is referred to as your non-dominant writing hand. Your non-dominant writing hand is connected to the right hemisphere of the brain while your dominant hand is connected to the left hemisphere of your brain.

Where your dominant hand tends to move fast, travelling speedily along familiar neural pathways, your non-dominant hand* puts a natural break on your thinking and writing. It slows things right down. When you connect with your right brain by using your non-dominant writing hand, it connects you with a different quality of thinking and thought processes.

According to William A Donius, author of *The Thought Revolution: How to unlock your inner genius* (2012), when you write with your non-dominant hand* you break the pattern of the familiar neural pathway to the brain that you follow when you write with your dominant hand. You're less likely to write the things you think you should write or say, and you're more likely to find a way to dig below the surface and come out with new and different thoughts and feelings. Try it right now. Take a clean page in your notebook and copy out the first paragraph of this chapter using your non-dominant writing hand. How is the shape of your writing different from your normal handwriting?

How did the pace feel to you? How legible are your sentences? Your sentences probably look very childlike – would you agree? Research has shown that writing with your non-dominant writing hand is likely to connect you with your inner child* and what it feels like to learn something from scratch, make mistakes, fail, and not get hung up on it. When children are allowed to freely express how they feel, there won't be a lot of editing going on and it's the same when you write with your non-dominant hand*. You'll access information and memories about yourself that stay locked away when you write with your dominant hand. While your dominant hand is more likely to write what you want to hear, the non-dominant hand* is likely to blurt out what you really feel. The left side of the brain rationalises and finds conclusions and justifications. The right brain, when activated through non-dominant handwriting, doesn't hold back the punches.

SEE ALSO
- **WAY 11: Why write by hand?** (page 46)
- **WAY 12: Write it down to make it happen** (page 48)

Hidden insights

There are plenty of hidden messages and insights awaiting you when you make use of writing with your non-dominant writing hand. Try this experiment, included by Donius (2012) in *The Thought Revolution* and reproduced here with permission.

At the top of a blank page in your notebook, write: '*If I were an animal, what kind of animal would I be?*'

Take a few seconds to think about your answer, then free write your response. Now switch your pen or pencil over to your non-dominant writing hand. Read the question again and take a few deep breaths before you begin. Using your non-dominant hand*, write your answer to the same question. Remember, this is not the time to worry about what your handwriting looks like.

Return to your dominant writing hand and reflect on what you wrote:

- Did you write about the same animal both times?
- If not, what do you notice about the differences between the two animals?
- Make a list of the characteristics of the animal(s) you recorded.
- Which of the characteristics do you share with the animal(s)?
- Which of the characteristics are more closely aligned to your true nature?
- Be on the look out for metaphors and similarities. For example, are there aspects of the animal's behaviour that are reflected in your own actions and behaviours?

Dogs, cats, horses and birds are the most common responses when people use their dominant writing hand. When it comes to the animals people connect with when using their non-dominant writing hand, however, the answers vary to a wider degree. The right side of the brain is more creative and intuitive in its thinking process. When I did this exercise using my dominant hand, the first animal I saw myself as was a bird. Using my non-dominant writing hand, the animal that came to me was a badger.

Donius believes that the first response is based on an aspirational view of ourselves, which is more connected to a rational, logical response. The second response is more likely to be a truer reflection of how you behave in normal everyday life. In other words, the second animal is a truer version of you.

What do you think? This is a great exercise to learn more about yourself. Try it out on other people and get them to come up with the animals they would use to describe both themselves and you, using both hands. It's interesting to see if there are synchronicities. Find out more about the medicine energy of the animals that are presented to you – you might enjoy Jamie Sams' *Medicine Cards*, a sacred guide to animal medicine (see http// jamiesams.org) or a free animal spirit guide reading from Dr Steven D Farmer's website (www.earthmagic.net).

WAY 14

Drawing is writing going deeper

'I believe that drawing lets you take that definition beyond the verbal, so it deep soaks into your mind and touches you to your reptilian core. Making pictures is pre-verbal so it brings enormous clarity.'
Danny Gregory, 2006 (artist and author)

Drawing pre-dates writing as a form of communication and was the first form of 'written' communication known to mankind. Drawing is as individual as handwriting and can be a powerful alchemist, extracting data from beyond the normal linear routes we access when making decisions.

You can also learn different things about yourself by drawing. When you draw, you often catch a glimpse of things that are missed by words. As you become a more attuned observer of your environment, yourself and others, you'll benefit greatly from the experience and deepen onto the page. The old adage 'a picture is worth a thousand words' may help you better understand this idea.

You don't need to be an artistic genius to draw or doodle in your notebook or journal.

One of the great things about drawing is that it doesn't have to be literal. Believe me, once you really start to see things, you'll be able to draw. Both drawing and writing can help you to be more present and observing of your environment and its contents.

Frederick Franck, painter, sculptor and author of *The Zen of Seeing: Seeing/drawing as meditation* (1973), writes about really drawing what we see and not what we just glance at. So much of the written word is about visuals. But think about how easy it is to go through your day oblivious to what is around you because you're not really taking things in. Franck understood this and his body of work has helped individuals move beyond looking to really seeing.

It's incredible to think about how much we don't see around us. We're overloaded with images, data and information that have stifled us and closed us down to really sensing and seeing our way through our day. Out in nature, we see what we think is a tree – but do we really see the unique design and textures of the tree's bark and the numerous shades of brown that colour her trunk? Do we already have an image of the tree in our consciousness before we've even examined it up close?

> **Tip:** In his book *The Creative License*, artist Danny Gregory (2006) presents an illuminating study of drawing, which really helps to validate its benefits. Gregory writes, *'Drawing in your journal is useful when you want to really get beneath an issue, or at a time when despite writing them out, the solutions and insights seem short in coming, then drawing may be the way to go.'*

Looking and seeing

How about trying to 'see beyond looking' as Franck suggests? Don't worry, there's no need to be good at drawing. To see does not require you to be an artist or even remotely talented; however, it does require a willingness to be open, to make mistakes and to give yourself permission to be imperfect.

You'll need pen or pencil, notebook or journal and an eraser (optional). Decide on the location where you'll carry out your practice.

Perform the alternate nostril breathing practice from **WAY 10: Stilling the mind to write** (page 42) before you begin. This is very important to do here as we sometimes have many, often negative, associations with drawing.

Decide what object you're going to engage with, then follow the instructions Franck gave to his students:

'Let your eyes fall on a subject in the room. Focus on it for a few minutes then close your eyes for five minutes. Open your eyes and focus on the same subject again. Look it straight in the eye. Really take it in as if it's the only object in the room.' (Franck, 1973)

According to Franck, once the 60 or more students in his class got past their initial reservations, they switched from looking to really seeing.

Free write or do more drawings about what you're really seeing.

Write now

Your writing will come alive when you clear the blockages that are getting in the way of you really seeing.

Your eyes are your individual lenses through which you view and see the world. It is these lenses that bring you to the page and render you sensitive to the energy of your interactions, your emotions and your feelings.

SEE ALSO
- **WAY 8: Visual writing prompts** (page 39)
- **WAY 13: Writing with your non-dominant hand** (page 50)

WAY 15 Writing the labyrinth

'Walking through the labyrinth activates different senses, in particular visual, auditory and kinesthetic ones.' A Monden, 2012

For most of your writing to wellness healing journey, I suggest that as far as possible, you complete your writing exercises by hand. There is no doubt that writing by hand is an ancient art and there is a close connection between the hand and your heart, as well as the other nervous centres in the body. You'll find more about this in **WAY 11: Why write by hand?** (page 46).

I'd now like to introduce you to an ancient tradition called walking the labyrinth, which you will use creatively on the page. Labyrinths predate Christianity and appear in all religions – the oldest known labyrinth existed more than 3,500 years ago on the Greek island of Crete. A labyrinth is not the same as a maze; it is a carefully designed winding, fluid path that people walk to gain mental and spiritual centring and healing. Earlier labyrinths were normally found outside, often carved in the earth, but labyrinths are now appearing in all sorts of places all over the world, including the famous labyrinth inside Grace Cathedral in San Francisco. We process more in a day than our ancestors would have processed in their whole lives – our lives have become complex and fast – and the intention behind the labyrinth is primarily to slow you down and move you towards a state of inner calm and greater clarity.

Other benefits of walking and writing your way around a labyrinth include transcending rational thinking, connecting the right and left brains and connecting with sacred geometry. The design of the labyrinth is based on sacred geometry, in which numbers and shapes have symbolic as well as numeric meaning.

Walking and writing the labyrinth has four distinct stages:

1. Your inward journey, where you're invited to enter the labyrinth with a specific question in mind.

2. The second stage brings you to the centre, where you're invited to stop and pause and make time for inner reflection. You can use your journal to write about what you're noticing and connecting with at this stage.

3. The return or outward journey. Here, you're invited to write with awareness outside the labyrinth about what occurred in the centre. Will it now help you move forward?

4. The final stage invites you to integrate the learning and insights from your writing walk outside the labyrinth. What will you be taking back with you into your everyday life?

SEE ALSO
- **WAY 16: Finger-walking the labyrinth** (page 58)
- **WAY 40: Writing with nature** (page 118)
- **WAY 41: Conversations with trees** (page 122)
- **WAY 42: Walking and writing** (page 126)

Into the labyrinth

Use the two blank labyrinths on pages 56 and 57 as your writing templates. You might want to make copies of these first, to use again in the future. Use the first one to write your way around to the centre of the labyrinth and the second one to write your way back out again. Using your pen as your guide, think of a problem or challenge you would like to take with you into the labyrinth. Before you begin, take a few minutes to sit quietly and perform the alternate nostril breathing practice you will find in **WAY 10: Stilling the mind to write** (page 42).

The symbolism of the labyrinth is very powerful. You'll be twisting and turning the page physically and moving your pen in the different directions that the path takes.

Writing in: Starting at the labyrinth entrance, write down your emotions and experiences about the challenge as you follow the path of the labyrinth around the page to the centre. Essentially, you are free writing your way around the labyrinth. As you follow the labyrinth path, make a note of any emotions or sensations that you feel. Write as fast or as slow as you like. When you arrive at the centre, if you feel there's more to write, either return to your notebook or free write around the edges of the labyrinth. When you have finished,

return your pen to the centre and rest a while. Sitting quietly, perhaps with your eyes closed, what do you notice, hear or feel? Notice the pace with which you wrote your way around the labyrinth. Was the pace fast or slow?

Writing out: Now you're ready for your return journey. Place your pen in the centre of the second labyrinth and write your way back from the centre, again following the paths until you arrive back at the entrance. You might be capturing ideas and solutions to your problem or challenge, or you could use the return journey to reflect on the process. Once you have arrived at the entrance, pause and then free write for 10 minutes about your experience.

Once you have walked the labyrinth on the page with your pen, why not take yourself outside for a walk? Going for a walk can be deeply grounding and soothing. According to life coach Karen Liebenguth (2012), *'When we're outside new insights emerge... It offers a chance to reconnect with nature and the seasonal energy to which our body, mind and soul are so closely connected.'* Find out whether there are any labyrinths in close proximity to where you live.

Write now

Writing out

WAY 16

Finger-walking the labyrinth

'Labyrinths are carefully designed to move you toward clarity or peace or at least a temporary calm. They are not unlike the human body in this way. We may not understand the purposes of all the internal parts, but they do their jobs.' M Garfield, 2002

Labyrinths are being used in a number of ways in everyday life. In medical centres, patients use them as a way to reflect and record their healing process. In prisons, they can be a place for quiet contemplation, and in churches and public spaces walking the labyrinth offers the opportunity for pilgrimages, spiritual restoration and community building. But what if you can't physically access or walk a labyrinth? Not to worry, walking a finger labyrinth can be just as effective.

In his 1999 article, *Off the Couch: An introduction to labyrinths and their therapeutic properties*, Neal Harris, a clinical professional counsellor, writes about the use of finger and walking labyrinths in his practice. His article points to research indicating how labyrinths positively affect brainwave activity, stimulating the alpha* and theta brainwave states and the neurological responses of some users. This has resulted in short-term increases in mental clarity in people with Alzheimer's disease, schizophrenia and dyslexia. It brings together the sensations of movement, touch and introspection on the page in a visceral way. Walking your own labyrinth is only a fingertip away.

SEE ALSO
- **WAY 15: Writing the labyrinth** (page 54)
- **WAY 40: Writing with nature** (page 118)
- **WAY 41: Conversations with trees** (page 122)
- **WAY 42: Walking and writing** (page 126)

A powerful walk

Use these guidelines to finger-walk your way around a labyrinth. The design of the labyrinth is inherently powerful as it is based on sacred geometry.

Prepare

- Print off a finger labyrinth from the Internet or use one of the templates from pages 56 and 57.

- Choose a quiet space, or you might want to play relaxing music in the background. Just make sure you can focus and won't be disturbed.

- Take a few deep breaths to clear your mind and place your labyrinth in front of you. Think about what you would like to contemplate as you finger-walk your way around the labyrinth. Bring your attention and focus to your index finger and the starting point of the labyrinth.

Readiness

- Take a moment to decide on a question you'd like some help with. Hold the question in your mind.

- Begin your walk from the entrance to the centre of the labyrinth along its pathways, using the middle finger of your non-dominant hand*. If using your non-dominant hand is awkward or uncomfortable, you can use the forefinger of your dominant hand instead – but remember, you're more likely to gain deeper insights when using your non-dominant hand.

Rest and reflect

- When you arrive at the centre, pause and rest for a while.

Receive

- Take a few moments to just be in the centre of the labyrinth with your thoughts and feelings. Observe what thoughts come into your mind. Bring your awareness to how you're feeling in your body. Are you feeling peaceful and calm? Are you feeling more centred?

Return

- Once you've sat quietly, noticing your feelings and emotions, you can prepare yourself for your return journey. Leaving the centre, use your non-dominant forefinger and finger walk your way back out of the labyrinth.

Record

- Once you have arrived back at the entrance, pause, take a few deep breaths and turn to your notebook and write down your insights and reflections.

- Sit back, take another deep breath and relax.

- Observe and write about how you feel.

Keep your finger labyrinth handy and finger-walk the labyrinth whenever you feel the need for more inner peace and self-realisation, or you're looking for a non-linear way to creative problem solving.

Write now

1 2 3 4 5 6 7 8
9 10 11 12 13 14
15 16 **17 18 19**
20 21 22 23 24
25 26 27 28 29
30 31 32 33 34
35 36 37 38 39
40 41 42 43 44
45 46 47 48 49

Chapter 3

MANAGING YOUR EMOTIONS: HOW TO WRITE FOR EMOTIONAL BALANCE

How we respond to our emotions can be a blueprint for our everyday actions and behaviours. Emotions can sometimes feel overwhelming but you will learn that it is more rewarding to face your emotions than take flight. This chapter will help you gain a better understanding of how emotions work and offer practical ways of handling emotions and beliefs that get in the way of your emotional, mental and often physical well-being. It will take you through identifying your specific moods, flushing out those core beliefs and identifying ways to give your emotional life balance through the 'Write now' practices. This chapter ends with a look at intuition* and how developing this sixth sense can help create a better you and help you make better choices and decisions by using your intuitive intelligence.

WAY 17

The shade of the shadow

'One does not become enlightened by imagining figures of light, but by making the darkness conscious.' Carl Jung (Jung *et al.*, 1983) (psychiatrist and psychotherapist)

Swiss psychologist and psychiatrist, Carl Jung (1875–1961) was responsible for coining the term 'the shadow*'. The shadow* can be described as those parts of the self that we feel bad about whether we're conscious or unconscious of the fact. We then project the denied shadow* aspects of our personality onto others. There is a life force and potency contained in the shadow* self. For many people, this is where their true voice is, where they may fully express themselves without a mask or without the rules and conditions of doing or saying the right thing. Writing is a safe and trusted method to write about your shadow*. It's safe to bring the shadow* self alive on the page. What you write won't be judged and it won't be ridiculed.

Writing honestly about your shadow* self is a way of moving the hidden aspects of the shadow* self from the dark into the light. Writing is a practical way of getting to know your shadow* more intimately. It won't feel so frightening when you allow the shadow* space to be expressed.

You might find that you feel more like yourself, that life feels more alive when you push past just wanting to show yourself and others your 'good' self. Think of it like this: often contained in the shadow* are some of the more natural parts of you, which are not contained or restricted by how you think you ought to be in the world. Imagine the freedom this might hold for you.

Consider this. Take three of your shadow* traits. Let's say one of your shadow* traits is selfishness. Consider a positive benefit of expressing more selfishness in your life. What might you gain from it? What if, by being selfish, you gave yourself the valuable time you need to rest rather than wearing yourself out being a social butterfly? Or perhaps your selfishness might protect your time, so you can get something important completed. Writers are fairly familiar with this.

SEE ALSO

- **WAY 18: The light of the shadow** (page 64)
- **WAY 35: Forgiveness (part 1)** (page 106)
- **WAY 36: Forgiveness (part 2)** (page 108)

Interview with your wild self

The following writing prompts invite you to conduct an interview with the wild (natural) shadow* parts of you.

- What would your wild self look like on the page?
- Give your shadow self a name.
- Describe the characteristics of the shadow self as if it were your best self.
- How would your shadow self be living his or her life?
- What would be different about their life compared to yours?
- What kind of home would they be living in?
- What foods would they eat?
- What kind of car would they drive?
- Describe the kinds of clothes they would wear.

- What is still unknown to you about this side of the self?

As you begin to define this character, see where bits of him or her show up in your everyday life. How could you further welcome parts of your shadow* into your everyday personality? The shadow* self is a vital part of who you are. When you find ways to accept and embrace this side of you, you no longer have to use your energy to push or resist the shadow's existence. This alone frees you up to think and act more creatively, from a place that is more whole and true to all the parts of you that make you who you are.

Write now

18 The light of the shadow

'Envy had a gift for me. It was green on one side, but gold on the other.'
Bonnie Friedman (author), 1995

Become your own therapist on the page. Seek out the ignoble parts of you and connect them with the noble parts. What could each of them learn form the other? How would a combination of both sides make a part of you stronger and more balanced? What might you discover and in many cases recover when you open up to the shadow* self?

Writing in his book, *The Gift of Therapy*, Irvin D Yalom (2001) encourages you to *'endeavour to normalise the shady side in any possible way. We therapists should be open to all our own dark, ignoble parts, and there are times when sharing them will enable patients to stop flagellating themselves for their own real or imagined transgressions.'*

How can you move from ignoble to noble? Well, this can be done by using your skill and wisdom to discover and recover the noble parts of your shadow* self. Very often it's considered to be the parts we're ashamed of that get hidden in the shadow, but in the shadow may also be parts of the self that are good, that have been left behind and are waiting to be reclaimed.

Draw two columns and make a list of your shadow* traits that you made in **WAY 17: The shade of the shadow** (page 62) in the left-hand column. Against each one, in the right-hand column, write down what

you get by expressing this part of your personality. In other words how does the shadow* self serve you?

For example:

Selfish	I have time for myself. I do what's important to me.
Mean	For the first time I'm being abundant with myself, so I can start saving for something that's important to me.
Messy	Means that I've allowed myself space and time to focus and work on one thing. I'll get to those other things in time.
Forgetful	I'm subconsciously forgetting the things I want to say no to. Now my next step is to say 'no' with respect and value for both me and the other person.

Now that you can see what you're getting from your shadow*, consider what you need to reclaim from your shadow* that might have been left behind.

When I shared this process with one of my clients, she found that she'd left behind the strong voice she'd had in childhood. By being told constantly to shut up as a child by her mother, she'd taken on a shadow* self that kept her thoughts to herself, not letting people know what she really thought. By reclaiming her voice, she suddenly found that she spoke out more, which brought her closer to others rather than pushing them away as she'd believed would happen.

Drawing out the shadow self

Try this writing practice to bring the shadow* self to the forefront.

Take a blank sheet of paper and divide it in half. On the right side of the page make a list of all your qualities and personality characteristics that you feel good about. Include all the things other people tell you they appreciate about you. Get as many items about the positive and loveable you into this column.

When you've finished, turn to the left side of the page. Think about the things you find difficult about you. What feels uncomfortable? What parts of the self do you hold back? What are the thoughts, actions or behaviours that you'd rather push to the side, overlook and not readily admit to? What do you hold back from others knowing about you? These may be things about yourself that don't make you feel good. Try your very best not to censor what you write. Be as honest as you can. Remember, these pages are private and for your eyes only. What would someone you don't get on with say about some of your less positive qualities? Include whatever else comes to mind in your left-hand column.

Next, write about the positive aspects of each of the shadow* aspects from your left-hand column, and find ways to express these more in your day-to-day interactions.

Take a short break. Put your papers down and take a quick walk or stretch. This is not just physical work, it's emotional work and looking after yourself is essential to maintaining your health and well-being. If you feel you need a longer time away from this list, by all means give yourself permission to do so. Go off and do something entirely different and return when you're ready.

Make sure that on your return, before you start any further work, you take four long deep breaths.

Write now

When you take ownership of your shadow*, it frees up your energy so you have more to expend in other areas of your life. You may even find that you start laughing at yourself as you loosen the grip on your shadow* aspects.

One of your biggest challenges will be in denying or pushing away the existence of the shadow* qualities in the left-hand column. By repressing or suppressing these emotions and feelings, you're siphoning off loads of energy from your vital alive self.

SEE ALSO
- **WAY 17: The shade of the shadow** (page 62)
- **WAY 35: Forgiveness (part 1)** (page 106)
- **WAY 36: Forgiveness (part 2)** (page 108)

WAY 19

Naming your emotions

'The most obvious difference is that emotions are much shorter than moods. Moods can last a whole day, sometimes two, while emotions can come and go in minutes.'
Paul Ekman (American psychologist), 2007

Angry	Sad	Depressed	Unmotivated
Tired	Energised	Depleted	Listless
Anxious	Nervous	Stressed	Fatigued
Cautious	Unsure	Stretched	Happy
Humiliated	Loving	Frustrated	Proud

One of the best ways of getting to grips with your emotions is to identify the emotions you're experiencing. By identifying your emotions and their triggers, you'll be in a more informed position to manage them. But recognising our moods and emotions is a tricky business. We receive mixed messages and get easily confused about what we really feel. The first step is to get more specific about your mood or emotion rather than generalising about how you think you feel. So rather than say, 'I feel bad today', be more specific about what the emotion is: 'I feel tired', 'I feel hungry', 'I feel demotivated', and so on. When you write your morning pages* or free writing exercises, open yourself to writing more specifically about what you feel. Get behind your feelings and tease them out on the page.

At the top of the next column is a range of emotions you're likely to experience. Add more in the blank boxes. By using one word to describe your emotions, you're more likely to get to the truer sense of what you're feeling. More than one word and your other thoughts are likely to have crept in.

Writing is a physical act, so understanding what you actually feel in your body will help you become more authentic on the page when it comes to identifying the cause of your moods and emotions.

Another way of becoming more observant about your moods is by listing three different emotions you experienced throughout your day, at the end of the day. You can check whether you've really captured the essence of your emotions by asking yourself, 'Is this really what I was feeling?'.

Think of a recent situation where you experienced a powerful or intense emotion. Capture the emotion using one word: _____ . Now write down the emotions you experienced during or immediately after being in that situation. Do this again, for five separate situations.

There are other ways to manage your emotions and moods. One option is to connect with nature and the changing seasons. Nature is a good reminder of the seasonal and cyclical changes in the body. Write about the weather as a free writing prompt. Learning to write no matter how you're feeling can be a motivator to manage your moods and emotions, whatever the weather.

Memories of aromas

Write now

Take a trip back down memory lane using your memories of food, smells or scents. Make a list of certain smells and scents from your childhood that bring back, strong, positive memories. Write about one of those memories in more detail. Think of ways to recreate the scents and smells you identified on your list to boost your moods. Plan a meal based on foods and flavours that invoke strong, positive memories from the past.

Keep a smells, scents and aroma diary: make a note in your notebook of the smells, scents or aromas you notice during the next seven days. What are your physical and emotional reactions to the smells and aromas you come into daily contact with. What smells invoke past memories? What scents are comforting? What aromas make you feel good? By knowing the impact of different scents, you can re-create aromas to lift your moods.

It is very easy to allow the mood you're in to stop you showing up on the page. The poet John Ashberry once told an interviewer, '*It is important to write when you are in the wrong mood or the weather is wrong. Even if you don't succeed you'll be developing a muscle that may do it later on*' (Sher, 1999). Don't wait for a gorgeous day to write about how great you feel. When it's cold and miserable, get yourself onto the page.

Another option is to gain a better understanding of the relationship between smell and your emotions. According to Dr Alan Hirsh, founder of the Smell and Taste Treatment and Research Foundation in Chicago, '*The quickest way to change someone's mood and behaviour is with smell, rather than with any other of our senses*' (Wollenberg, 2011).

I came across a lovely memory from Val Monroe, the beauty editor at *Oprah* magazine, who retells an experience of attending a

launch for a new fragrance. She dabs one of the perfumes on her wrist and, in an instant, a memory of her cousin Ruth who gave her piano lessons when she was five emerges, '*fully forward, her grey hair perfectly coiled into a French twist, her black wool, fitted sheath meticulously pressed, her Ferragamo pumps shiny and new. Cuir de Russire had been her fragrance and I never knew that till I smelled it the other day*' (Monroe, 2007).

You too can recall certain memories or smells to invoke positive memories and use those smells and connections to boost your mood.

SEE ALSO
- **WAY 20: Capturing your core beliefs** (page 68)
- **WAY 21: Discounting your core beliefs** (page 71)
- **WAY 22: Blocked emotions** (page 74)
- **WAY 23: A paper ritual for releasing your emotions** (page 76)

WAY 20 Capturing your core beliefs

'Loving ourselves is no easy matter, because it means loving all of oneself, including the shadow where one is inferior and socially so unacceptable.' James Hillman (psychologist) (Schwartz, 2011)

A core belief is a belief you probably formed as a result of one of your earlier, traumatic childhood experiences. While some core beliefs can be positive, the ones I'm referring to here are negative core beliefs. Core beliefs result in you constructing an absolute belief about yourself, others and the world. A core belief might be not believing in yourself. It might manifest in your believing that you're a bad person; or it could be based on the early death of a parent, resulting in a core belief that the people you love abandon you. What makes it a core belief is that it is likely to have happened at a young age when you were less discerning and didn't have the ability to evaluate your experiences fully.

SEE ALSO

- **WAY 9: Inner wise writing self** (page 40)
- **WAY 21: Discounting your core beliefs** (page 71)
- **WAY 23: A paper ritual for releasing your emotions** (page 76)
- **WAY 35: Forgiveness (part 1)** (page 106)
- **WAY 36: Forgiveness (part 2)** (page 108)

Working with your core beliefs

In the privacy of your notebook, quick-think as many examples as you can of your own personal core beliefs. They often show up in the kind of things you say about yourself in your head, or your perception of how you perceive yourself. Your core beliefs show up in the limitations you place on yourself in terms of what you must do, should do; the rules and expectations you have of yourself and others.

Make a list of what you know to be your main core beliefs about yourself. To begin with, your list may not be huge, which is why it's a good idea to generate this list over a few days. Once you have at least seven core beliefs on your list, you're ready to move onto the next step.

- Choose one of the core beliefs from your list and write it across the top of a new page. How far back can you trace the origins of this belief?
- Most of your core beliefs stem from early childhood, but some can also result from

your adult experiences. What are some of your more recent core beliefs that have stemmed from your adult life?

- Take a new page in your notebook and write a short story describing your first meeting with this core belief. How old were you when first you met? Where did you meet? Who else was there? What were the circumstances that brought you both together? What did you believe as a result of meeting up with this core belief?

- Write the ending of the story based on the outcomes on your life as a result of you believing in this core belief 100 per cent. Be very specific about the ways the core belief has impacted on your life and your behaviours.

- Free write your reflections on what you have written.

WAY 21 Discounting your core beliefs

'You can transcend all negativity when you realise that the only power it has over you is your belief in it. As you experience this truth about yourself, you are set free.'
Eileen Caddy (Co-founder of Findhorn)
(Armstrong, 2008)

Your core beliefs involve very tricky emotions. They're very good at appearing as if what they say to you is absolutely true. Earlier I said it would take time to work on shifting these beliefs, and I want you to hold this as true when you work through the next few chapters. After all, your beliefs have had years to deeply embed themselves into your way of being and are deeply entrenched. Even if you're intellectually aware of the negative impact of your core beliefs, you may still act is if they're true because it all feels way too familiar. But one way you can begin to dismantle a core belief is by disputing the very 'evidence' it has got away with fobbing you off with.

You might find it helpful to use New Supporting Beliefs cards – I have filled in an example on page 72, and provided a blank template for you to complete on page 73. These cards provide space where you can you make written records of all the real evidence that disproves your old core belief. Your task will be to record even the smallest pieces of evidence – even those that appear trivial –

that dispute your old core belief and put the spotlight on the evidence that supports your new belief. Over time, your collected data will add weight to the untruths of the old core belief. Remember, your new supporting belief doesn't have to be the direct opposite of one of your earlier negative core beliefs. So a core belief of 'I'm not good enough' doesn't suddenly turn into 'I'm a great and loveable human being'; instead, it could become something like, 'I'm worth spending 10 minutes every day focused on me'.

Keep referring back to the evidence of your New Supporting Belief card. Your shifts may not happen overnight but, over time, the more you make a habit of writing down and referring back to the evidence, things will change.

Remember, you've developed and to a great extent mastered the skill of recalling the memories of your negative experiences and using them to confirm and reinforce your negative core beliefs. With this new approach in place, you're laying down new tracks and focusing and directing your energies differently, in the direction of the positive. Be patient with this work.

SEE ALSO
- **WAY 9: Inner wise writing self** (page 40)
- **WAY 10: Stilling the mind to write** (page 42)
- **WAY 19: Naming your emotions** (page 66)
- **WAY 22: Blocked emotions** (page 74)
- **WAY 23: A paper ritual for releasing your emotions** (page 76)

New supporting belief: I am worth spending 10 minutes every day focused on me

I felt better writing in my journal today even though I had a stressful day at work. In fact, it helped me cope with the challenges much better.

Date: 5 September

I find that I'm looking forward to those 10 minutes in the morning and I often find myself writing for longer.

Date: 8 September

It's really helping, writing about how I'm feeling. I'm sometimes surprised at the things that crop up on the page.

Date: 10 September

Carrying a smaller notebook means I'm writing in my journal at other times of the day. Today I wrote at lunchtime for 10 minutes then went for a 10-minute walk around the block. I felt relaxed and energised.

Date: 11 September

I noticed how awful I felt today because I missed my morning session because of the early morning train I need to catch. I could have written on the train.

Date: 15 September

I was able to go back into my journal and remind myself about what I said I didn't want from a certain relationship. It felt good seeing it in black and white, and also knowing that it didn't have to stay that way forever.

Date: 16 September

Writing out three good things I appreciated about my day really shifted how I was feeling this evening. I must do this practice more often. I think it helped me to have a much better sleep.

Date: 17 September

I wrote for five minutes today about the difficult conversation I had with my boss. It wasn't as bad as I thought it was. I could see how I made a stand for myself and didn't collapse under her criticism.

Date: 20 September

I remembered those quotes I'd captured in my journal last week and was able to share it with my friend last night who was going through a difficult time.

Date: 22 September

One of my colleagues commented today on how much calmer and self-assured I seem these days and mentioned that other people had said the same thing too.

Date: 24 September

For the last four days I have been really busy and missed journaling, but re-reading this support card has reminded me of just how much I get from taking 10 minutes to spend with myself.

Date: 29 September

I've worked out that over this last month I've invested over 280 minutes focusing on me. This is a huge revelation and shift for me. I want to double this over the next few months.

Date: 30 September

Write now

New supporting belief

Date:

Date:

Date:

Date:

Date:

Date:

Date:

Date:

Date:

WAY 22 Blocked emotions

'As writers we must be willing to feel our sadness, our anger and terror, so we can reach in and find our sweet vulnerability...'
Nancy Slonim Aronie, 1998 (author)

We block emotions for different reasons; some are automatic and some are driven by the unconscious. We're not always ready to process or face up to certain emotions, depending on whatever is going on at the time in our lives. Sometimes, you're literally building up your mental and physical reserves until the right moment arises. And sometimes blocking is done to help you pace yourself, so you're not overwhelmed with difficult feelings all at the same time.

Blocked emotions become a problem when they're stacked up or when you're totally unaware of their presence. Storing up your emotions and holding them at bay means there's a possibility of the emotions leaking out and having their say anyway. Being unaware of this causes even more havoc. Unchecked emotions will often find other ways of finding a release or outlet, often when least expected and often in self-destructive ways.

Very often, these emotions will have been stopped in their tracks or had their natural flow interrupted. With their release put on hold, it's likely that the feelings will be contained in a space that's not big enough to hold the emotional charge or energy of your feelings.

In a conscious state, we can deliberately suppress and hold back feelings that we're not ready to deal with, such as shame or humiliation. In an unconscious state, we may fall into repressing our feelings when dealing with any emotional material. The trick is to sharpen your awareness around when you block your emotions and to be mindful of not doing it too often or for too long.

The regular practice of free writing and writing morning pages* is a good space to offload and connect with some of your unconscious and repressed feelings. By relaxing and going with the flow, the unconscious will find its way through to the surface. These are the moments when feelings you didn't realise you had or felt emerge, and where surprises and new discoveries are made. Writing is, in many respects, an act of courage.

There's a real cost to burying emotions, which can result in physical and emotional symptoms. In her book *Writing for Emotional Balance*, Beth Jacobs (2004) quotes research by Muraven and Baumeister from 2000, that concluded that the effort to suppress feelings costs individuals measurable energy. This energy loss can result in a decrease in mental and physical stamina, problems with the functioning of the immune system or slower recovery from pain.

Discovering your emotional blockages

Try this way to discover where you are emotionally blocked.

- In what situations do you have difficulty in expressing how you're really feeling?
- What emotions or feelings get blocked as a result?
- What activities do you resort to in order to avoid feeling the blocked emotions or feelings?
- What are the concrete signs that signpost to you that you're in an emotionally blocked state?
- Begin to generate a list of alternative responses to blocking or holding back your emotions.

Writing your journal gives you a regular and consistent method for tracking and checking up on the signs that you might be falling into the trap of becoming emotionally blocked. Use the exercises from **WAY 19: Naming your emotions** (page 66) to identify the emotions you feel throughout your day. If you miss a few days writing in your journal and haven't checked in with your emotions, don't worry, wait until you're engaged in a regular, repetitive activity, such as loading the dishwasher or taking a shower, that frees up your head space to reflect on the previous day and the emotions you felt.

Write now

SEE ALSO
- **WAY 23: A paper ritual for releasing your emotions** (page 76)
- **WAY 35: Forgiveness (part 1)** (page 106)
- **WAY 36: Forgiveness (part 2)** (page 108)
- **WAY 45: Our bodies, ourselves** (page 132)
- **WAY 46: Body stories** (page 134)

23

A paper ritual for releasing your emotions

'Tidied up all my papers. Tore up and ruthlessly destroyed much. This is always a great satisfaction.' Katherine Mansfield (writer) (Breathnach, 1995)

Expressing and getting rid of your emotions on paper is one way of releasing them. The journal or notebook is the perfect place for downloading your secrets or things about your life, experiences or relationships that trigger feelings of shame, embarrassment or humiliation. All those emotions that don't leave you feeling good. But once on the page, how useful is it to leave some of your secrets behind?

One idea is to plan regular rituals or ceremonies to release your words. It's great that you are no longer keeping the lid on how you feel – and it can be equally liberating to ceremoniously let them go. Explore the different options for releasing your words with a bit of ritual.

SEE ALSO
- **WAY 6: Writing habits and rituals** (page 32)
- **WAY 19: Naming your emotions** (page 66)
- **WAY 22: Blocked emotions** (page 74)
- **WAY 35: Forgiveness (part 1)** (page 106)
- **WAY 36: Forgiveness (part 2)** (page 108)

Releasing ritual

On a loose sheet of paper, free write your feelings on these writing prompts to help you really explore and unpack your feelings:

- Put a secret you've never shared with anyone onto the page and see how it feels.
- What are three emotions you feel ashamed of or feel guilty about feeling?
- Which one was the most difficult to own up to?
- What's it like to feel and own up to this emotion?
- What's the most awful thing you feel associated with this emotion?
- When was the last time you felt this emotion and what were the circumstances?
- What triggers or connects you to feeling this emotion?
- Why are you secretly ashamed of having this emotion?
- My most hated and shameful emotion is...

Now you're going to ceremoniously get rid of what you've just written. It's out on the page now so let's add a sense of ritual and ceremony as a way of making this meaningful and of value. What would be the best release method for you?

Write now

You could...

- Squeeze the paper into a tight ball and toss it ceremoniously into a rubbish bin.
- Tear it up into tiny shreds. Now you've not only dissected every word but also demolished every letter. You can dispose of it by:
  - flushing it away
  - placing it in a bottle and sending it out to sea
  - mailing it to a fictional address with no return details
  - disposing of it in the rubbish
  - burying it outside in the earth
  - scattering it into the air on a windy day.
- Take it outside, set the page alight and watch it burn, then return the ashes to the earth.
- Run water over the page and watch the ink bleed the words away and the paper disintegrate into a soggy mess.
- Roll the paper up into a ball, throw it on the floor and repeatedly stamp on it. Imagine yourself crushing the emotions to death.

Choose the release ritual that feels right for you. When you've finished, give yourself a small treat to acknowledge the ritual release you've just been a part of.

WAY 24 Intuition – your inner wisdom

'Between the conscious and the unconscious, the mind has put up a swing.'
The Kabir Book, **Robert Bly's translation of a 15th century Indian mystic (Harris, 2001)**

Intuition* is the wisest internal advisor you'll ever have. Sometimes referred to as our 'inner tuition', it's the science of knowing without having tangible, concrete evidence in advance of a situation or occurrence happening. Your intuitive intelligence often happens beyond the limits of the rational and logical brain, and writing is one way of really gathering the evidence that your intuition* works.

Closely connected to an intricate system of sensory organs in the body, your intuition* is more of a sensed feeling, sometimes referred to as the sixth sense – an advanced system of sensing that incorporates hearing, seeing, smell, taste and touch, and that goes beyond all five senses.

Two recent studies – one at the University of Iowa and the other at the Medical Research Council in the UK – found that patients responded physically to a rigged deck of cards long before they'd rationally worked out what was happening (Murphy, 2011). Signs included players showing early stress responses to the rigged decks, plus a dip in the players' heart rates whenever they went near certain decks. The studies demonstrated that the body was giving signals long before the conscious mind had made the connections.

Another study, in 2005, found that our sensitivity to the body's signals and intuitive tracking is greatly enhanced following the experience of meditation. Recent research in neuroscience* indicates that if an intuitive insight (or any new idea) is not captured within 37 seconds, it is likely never to be recalled again. In their book *The Success Principles* (2006), Jack Canfield and Janet Switzer suggest that in seven minutes it's gone forever.

When I was 26 years old and heavily pregnant with my daughter, I was staying at my parents' home as I was close to giving birth. One morning I woke up from a strong dream that was very specific and detailed. I couldn't shake the content of the dream, which was insistent on my getting up as quickly as I could and travelling across south London to my home. On that particular day none of my family was at home so I had no one to question or check out the strong urge I had, so I followed my intuition* and slowly made my way across town to my home. As I put the key in the front door I knew something was not right. All my senses heightened, even though I couldn't quite rationalise what I was connecting with. To cut a long story short, my flatmate had left the bath running – it was full to the brim with water and just about to spill over. It would have resulted in severe damage to the flat. I saved my home from damage by following my intuition* and the powerful message from my dream. My daughter was born naturally the next day.

Hopefully, *49 Ways To Write Yourself Well* is enabling you to slow down the pace in your busy and hectic daily life. The more relaxed, quiet and still we are, the more able we are to tune into our intuitive intelligence.

Working with your inner wisdom

Everyone has an intuition* story. What's yours? Writing it down can give it greater legitimacy. Spend some time exploring in your notebook your personal experiences of intuition*.

What has been the most remarkable intuitive experience you've ever had? Write it out as if you were relaying the experience to a stranger. Be aware of the signs and signals that made the experience come alive.

One way to deepen this extra sensory skill is to notice when your intuition* kicks in and when it comes up trumps. Make a note of when you responded to an intuitive response that was correct.

How reliable were your judgements? How many times did your intuition* turn out to be anxiety or nerves? What was the difference between the signals in the two responses? Look out for the more subtle signals and clues. How can you improve on your intuitive judgement?

Try this experiment for one week. As you go through your day, write down all the examples where you get a feeling about something. At the end of the week, notice which of your feelings turned out to be right. This is the process of logging your intuitions before they're censored by rational analysis.

SEE ALSO

- **WAY 9: Inner wise writing self** (page 40)
- **WAY 10: Stilling the mind to write** (page 42)
- **WAY 13: Writing with your non-dominant hand** (page 50)

1 2 3 4 5 6 7 8
9 10 11 12 13 14
15 16 17 18 19
20 21 22 23 24
25 26 27 28 29
30 31 32 33 34
35 36 37 38 39
40 41 42 43 44
45 46 47 48 49

Chapter 4

THERAPY ON THE PAGE: THERAPEUTIC MODELS TO CHALLENGE YOUR THOUGHTS AND BELIEFS

There is much to be gained from traditional therapy that will help you gain insights into yourself. This chapter combines powerful techniques from psychology, therapy and coaching and introduces therapeutic models and theories that you can use quickly to process and gain insights into your relationships with others and your own actions and behaviours. With regular practice, alongside your free writing and morning pages*, you will build and develop your own inner wise writing self* as you gain greater perspective on your relationships with yourself and others.

Each of the 'Write now' practices in this chapter shows you, the 'author', how to take charge of your own learning and growth by embedding these techniques as writing practices that will become second nature to you.

You will be shown how to use the rational emotive behavioural therapy ABCDE model to confront your beliefs if you are experiencing self-doubt or a lack of confidence. Not sure what impact positive and negative words hold in writing? This chapter will teach you about research that highlights the importance of balance in the use of negative and positive words when writing about traumatic events. Having a conflict with a colleague or family member? The chapter explores the neuro-linguistic programming (NLP) model of perceptual positions. You will learn about life scripts, drivers and the Karpman Drama Triangle*, all of which are models and theories originating from transactional analysis work.

The chapter ends with a focus on a set of transformational questions that you can try out on yourself to self-coach your way from problem to solution. This chapter will help you to better understand the dynamic and interpersonal relationships between you and others and between others and yourself, and interpersonal communication in groups in both formal and informal settings.

WAY 25 Challenge your beliefs

'Thoughts are like seeds. As are my thoughts, so will be my attitude and behaviour. Therefore my focus shouldn't be so much on wrong behaviour as on the thinking which causes it.' D Janki, 2010

Did you know that negative beliefs are the number one block to maintaining thriving health and well-being? Negative beliefs are not supportive and can hold you back in so many ways. What helps is knowing a bit about how beliefs work and how to put into practice tools and techniques that will help dismantle your limiting beliefs in a constructive way.

One method, which is probably one of the most widely used therapies in the world, is the rational emotive behavioural therapy (REBT) pioneered in the 1950s by psychologist Dr Albert Ellis. REBT is a practical approach to challenging beliefs using the power of our cognitive and writing skills.

Challenging your beliefs before you write will help you really tap into your inner creative resources. Negative beliefs left untapped have enormous potential to sabotage any attempts you may make in moving and progressing your writing in a productive and positive way.

SEE ALSO
- **WAY 20: Capturing your core beliefs** (page 68)
- **WAY 21: Discounting your core beliefs** (page 71)

Imagine your beliefs as a pair of glasses. When you wear one particular pair of glasses you see life and events from your life in a particular light. Through these lenses, no matter what is happening, you see what you view as good and positive. But through another set of glasses, the view can be far from rosy. In fact, everything is distorted with a particular meaning, which renders us powerless over our circumstances.

It's the view of our events that can cause us harm rather than the event itself. Dr Ellis created the ABCDE model to show how our beliefs impact on our emotional responses and behaviours.

The ABCDE model

Grab your pen and notebook, and work through the steps of the ABCDE model:

- **A** stands for the Activation or event that was the original or key event where you first adopted this belief.

- **B** stands for the Belief you have as a result of your interpretation of the event. What was your interpretation of the event and what belief did you come away with?

- **C** highlights the Consequences and impact this particular belief now has on your life, through your habits, thoughts about yourself and behaviours. A doesn't cause C; it's B that causes C, and this is where the work needs to be done.

- **D** is where you examine the belief much more closely and identify even the smallest of evidence that Denies, Disputes or Disagrees with your belief. It challenges what you believe to be true.

- **E** stands for the Effects and how you now feel as a result of changing or shifting your beliefs, as well as identifying how it feels to gain a different perspective of the old belief.

A final question to complete the model would be to ask yourself: 'What is available to me now that I no longer hold onto this belief?'.

It's important to see your responses in writing rather than just mulling them over in your head. Dr Ellis believes that the real work lies in the recognition that we don't need to cling to our irrational beliefs – but it takes practice, practice and practice. Changing your beliefs is a powerful catalyst in changing the outcome: recognising that shit happens but how we view the event is what makes the difference.

Everyone has his or her good points; and weak points lead us to embed and embody self-acceptance. REBT is an easy tool to reduce emotional pain. It may not get rid of all of your negative beliefs, but it can significantly reduce the frequency with which you allow your irrational beliefs to drive your behaviour.

Write now

WAY 26 Word rehab

'I like good strong words that mean something.' **Louisa May Alcott, 2005 (author of *Little Women*)**

In this 'Way', we're going to take a problem or challenge you currently have and give it a different kind of makeover.

Studies and research documented in *The Secret Life of Pronouns* (Pennebaker, 2012) documented six writing studies that yielded some unexpected results. Overall, the more that people used positive emotions while writing about emotional upheavals, the more their physical and mental health improved in the weeks and months after the experiment.

Those who expressed high levels of negative emotions didn't benefit from the writing. However, whereas physical health improved for people who used a moderate number of negative emotion words, people who didn't use negative words at all – perhaps failing to really acknowledge their feelings – didn't benefit from the writing either.

The findings from the studies suggest that to gain the most benefit from writing about difficult or traumatic events, you need to both acknowledge the negative and celebrate the positive.

SEE ALSO
- **WAY 25: Challenge your beliefs** (page 82)

~~Negatives~~ Positives!

Transforming the negatives

Take 10 minutes and write a full description of a challenge or problem you have. Write about how you feel about it, what caused it, who's to blame – whatever comes to mind; just get it down on the page.

Now, using a different colour of pen, circle or underline every single word or sentence that has a negative or painful association. You're plucking out those words on the page that have negative energy. Assemble all the words or sentences on a blank page in a new list. Don't worry if you find you've repeated the whole of your blurb. This will reinforce the learning even more. Once you've finished, run your eye down that list. What do you notice and feel about all the words and sentences on your list?

Studies have shown that when we see words associated with a particular ailment or emotion, we tend to become the word. So when we see words associated with anger we become rude and when we see words associated with sadness our feelings of depression increase. The psychological title given to this response is 'affective priming'. But affective priming is a double-edged sword. It doesn't just work negatively, it also works positively, which is why we can account for the abundance of affirmations in the self-help movement. The roots of affirmations lie in affective priming.

This exercise really demonstrates the power of the pen: you now have the power in your hands to transform every negative word in your dialogue into something more empowering, liberating and encouraging. Start rewriting what you have written about your challenge. For example, the words 'not sure' could become 'open to possibilities'. The words 'can't think of what to do' become 'there are many options I can consider'. 'It shouldn't happen to me' becomes 'I'm more resourceful than I think'.

Now take a look at your newly scripted challenge. What does your energy feel like now? How motivated are you to face your challenge with new vigour and possibilities? Take a moment to record what you notice in your journal.

Write now

27 Trading places

'Writing can't change the story, but it can change how you think about it.'
J Connor, 2008

Movement can be a powerful catalyst for changing how we feel. The act of writing requires movement. Becoming more of an observer in your life and using writing to capture your observations can provide you not only with insights but also with new ways of viewing difficult and challenging situations.

Let's take a difficult relationship you're having with someone, either at work or at home. We'll be using a model called perceptual positions*, which was pioneered by psychologists Judith DeLozier and John Grinder. A common model widely used in neuro-linguistic programming (NLP), perceptual positions invites you to explore a particular situation or event from three different perspectives – or, you could say three different points of view.

SEE ALSO
- **WAY 31: A walk around the Karpman Triangle** (page 94)

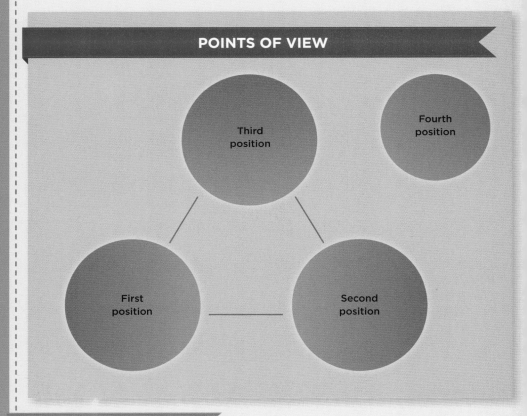

POINTS OF VIEW

Third position

Fourth position

First position

Second position

Exploring different positions

Grab your notebook and on a blank page, draw three separate circles, one at each corner of a triangle. Label the circles 'First position', 'Second position' and 'Third position'.

We'll start with the first position. This covers your personal experience of the relationship or event you'll be exploring. For the next five minutes, write a detailed description of your viewpoint of the situation or relationship. How do you see it? What's your take on the situation? Write your description in the first person.

Now, move on to the second position. Here, it is your turn to stand in the shoes of the person you're having a conflict or difficulty with. Writing in the second person and using the person's name, imagine how and what this person must be feeling. What and how do things look like from where they're standing? What might you have missed or overlooked? What are you now able to get a better handle on that was distorted from the view and experience of the first position? Write in as much detail as you can for five minutes. Take another short break.

Now turn your focus to the third position. This is the place of what is called the impartial observer. Imagine that you're able to understand both sides of the story objectively, that you're able to see and connect with things that may have been missed by the other two positions. This is also the position of the wise advisor.

From this position, write about what your wise self would see and share about the situation, with a view to helping both individuals resolve the situation. Writing with your non-dominant writing hand is a great way to access the wisdom of this position. Write in as much detail as you can about what the observer sees, hears and feels from this position.

Once you've completed this, give yourself five minutes to allow the reflections from your writing to process and unravel in your mind. Now draw a new circle and label it 'Fourth position'. What is the learning and wisdom that you now recognise, having explored all three positions? What new insights have you gained? What actions will you now take? What will you now do differently? Take five minutes and gather your thoughts and reflections on paper.

Sometimes we can get stuck in one of the positions. An individual stuck in the first position only sees things through their own eyes. Someone stuck in the second position can often see things mostly from the viewpoint of others. And being stuck in the third position might find you coming across as aloof and distant, as the outsider looking in. All three positions are of equal value and being conscious of each of them can be empowering as we interact with others throughout our day. The fourth position is a valuable place to gather and acknowledge all that you're learning.

Write now

28 Parent, child, adult ego states

'The family we are born into is life's greatest lottery, but they are not our only tribe.'
Susannah Conway, 2012

Have you ever found yourself screaming at someone like a two-year-old child because they got you so mad? Chances are you're in one of the three ego states that form the core foundation of transactional analysis*.

The first is the parent ego state where much of our learned behaviour may have been modelled from earlier childhood relationships with parents and adults. The parent ego state is often associated with 'shoulds', guilt, punishment or condemnation on all levels and degrees. The parent ego state has two modes: controlling parent and nurturing parent. It contains values, rules, social conditioning and many things that we modelled from our parents and other powerful adults. The adult ego state can be nurturing and supportive, offer guidance and provide safe limits and boundaries (the nurturing parent). Or it can be critical, punitive, blaming, shaming or judgemental (the critical parent).

At the opposite end of the spectrum is the child ego state. Here, we re-experience strong emotions and desires, such as fear, anger, joy and delight. The child ego state contains the emotions, feelings, needs and wishes we experienced as children. It contains the

decisions we made about the world as a result of not having our emotional or physical needs met. The child can either be adapted (compliant, sulky and obedient) or natural (spontaneous, creative and playful).

The third ego state, which is often represented in between the parent and child ego states, is the adult ego state. In this state, we are operating in the here and now. We have the ability to process more rationally and make decisions about how to act. This results in more mature, non-judgemental and logical behaviour.

Where thing gets tricky is when communication between the states becomes what Dr Eric Berne refers to as 'crossed' (Phillips, 2005). For example:

Your partner: *'Where are my glasses?'* (Adult request)
Your response: *'Why don't you look after your things instead of always relying on me?'* (Controlling parent response).

An alternative response, such as *'The last time I saw them they were in the bathroom – is there somewhere you can leave them that would make it easier to locate them when you can't find them?'* comes from the adult ego state. What you're looking for is an adult-adult response.

SEE ALSO
• **WAY 29: I'm OK and you're OK** (page 90)

Crossed communication

Let's explore Dr Berne's 'crossed' communication between the states in more detail. You'll need three different coloured pens or markers for this activity.

- Think about two difficult conversations you have had, either recently or in the past. Write out the dialogue of each in your notebook in as much detail as you can recall.

- Next, go through the dialogue sentence by sentence and at the end of each exchange write what ego state the response was most likely coming from.

- Using a different coloured pen or marker, write in a series of alternative responses, where the reply is more reflective of an adult-adult response.

- What are you noticing about the exchange now?

- What helps you to respond more from your adult ego state?

Write now

THE EGO STATES

PARENT EGO STATE
Behaviours, thoughts and feelings copied from parents or parent figures

ADULT EGO STATE
Behaviours, thoughts and feelings that are direct responses to the here and now

C

CHILD EGO STATE
Behaviours, thoughts and feelings replayed from childhood

WAY 29 I'm OK and you're OK

'*Most of the shadows of this life are caused by standing in our own sunshine.*'
Ralph Waldo Emerson (writer) (Noble, 2012)

What does your life script say about how you view life? In the 1960s, after parting ways with Freud and becoming despondent about the therapies around at the time, Canadian psychiatrist and psychoanalyst Dr Eric Berne founded an interesting therapeutic approach called transactional analysis*. TA, as it's commonly known, is rooted in three main assumptions and principles:

- People are OK and we are all equals, regardless of status and difference.

- Everyone has the capacity to think and make choices. You are responsible for yourself and make choices all the time
- You can decide to change. You have autonomy whatever the situation. You're not compelled to live out the life of an unsatisfactory childhood

Dr Berne's hypothesis is that people form a 'script', which is essentially an individual's belief about who they are, what the world is like, how they relate to the world, how the world relates to them and how others treat them. Out of this thinking, Thomas Harris, an early contributor to TA, developed the life scripts* or life positions model. This model offers a way of understanding what position we're taking when we think negatively about ourselves.

SEE ALSO
- **WAY 28: Parent, child, adult ego states** (page 88)

THE FOUR LIFE POSITIONS

You're OK with me

I'm not OK You're OK	I'm OK You're OK
Get away from 'Helpless'	Get on with 'Happy'
I'm not OK You're not OK	I'm OK You're not OK
Get nowhere with 'Hopeless'	Get rid of 'Angry'

I'm not OK with me

I'm OK with me

You're not OK with me

Your life positions

Draw a box like the one opposite, containing four equal squares. Add the main labels as shown:

- I'm OK, You're OK (sometimes referred to as the 'get on with' position)
- I'm OK, You're not OK (sometimes referred to as the 'get rid of' position)
- I'm not OK, You're not OK (sometimes referred to as the 'get nowhere with' position)
- I'm not OK, You're OK (sometimes referred to as the 'get away from' position).

I bet you've already had a reaction to one or more of these boxes. Perhaps a particular box has reminded you of a specific event and how you might have responded and felt? Write about the event and your feelings for five minutes before you move onto the next stage.

Now we're going to work through writing and exploring different scenarios and events associated with each of the different boxes.

I'm OK, you're OK: This is the ideal, the box where you want to be most located in your life. From this position, not only do you have respect for yourself but you also have respect from others. You see yourself and others as equal, regardless of race, gender, income or position. You define success on your own terms. Decisions made from this place are more empowering and enduring, even though this may involve personal exposure or vulnerability and knowing that others may not agree with how you think or feel. Write about a time when you felt okay and you felt that others were okay too.

I'm OK, you're not OK: Writing about this box may feel a little more challenging. It's important to be honest here. Where in your life have you behaved in a way where you felt you were okay and another person was not okay? You may remember examples of where as a child you had to hit back to survive and you still use that position in the way you communicate or challenge others.

I'm not OK, you're OK: Think back to a time when you believed that others were cleverer, more popular, more beautiful or more important than you were. Perhaps to compensate for this feeling, you've been on a running treadmill of accumulating awards and qualifications to justify your worth. Think of a situation and write about it. How does 'you're okay and I'm not' show up in your life?

I'm not OK, you're not OK: You may have felt helpless and powerless at different points in your life. You may have believed that you're doomed to fail – and the thing that you've believed has in fact happened. Write about one of these situations. How did it feel?

Now consider the four life positions.

- Which of them is your default position?
- Which of them are your peers demonstrating?
- What would need to change for you to operate more from the 'I'm OK, you're OK' life position?

Knowing your life positions can help you consider your behaviour and decide how and what you want to change.

WAY 30

What are your emotional drivers?

'Once we notice the places in our lives where we've kept these emotional patterns alive we can shake ourselves out of our complacency and reassess who we are, as our old conditioning, our old sense of self is challenged.' Tara Bennett-Goleman, 2003 (psychotherapist)

We develop defences and ways of protecting ourselves against the negatives inherited from our early childhood experiences. Building on the original work of Dr Eric Berne, Taibi Kahler and Hedges Capers developed the concept of drivers or mini scripts. Kahler and Capers identified five major life scripts* that emerge as a result of the messages we take on from parents, other adults and the dominant culture. We use these messages to push and drive and berate ourselves. The initial intention of a driver is to help you work more effectively. But, in the course of your relationship with the drivers you adopt, this is turned on its head and the driver turns into a stick with which you beat yourself.

You might well be wondering what is wrong with having a driver as long you get the job done. This is a good question to ask, and it's useful to explore your drivers. Because of their driven nature, they often lack spontaneity and creativity – the qualities you need lots of on your Write Yourself Well journey. Being driven also stops you from taking time out to pause, reflect and be fully present in your day.

Have a look through this list of five of the most common drivers. Which one do you most identify with?

1. The **be perfect** driver pushes you to do things perfectly, often first time without mistakes, and you can also have those expectations of others; this, in turn, can be hard on those around you.

2. The **be strong** driver makes you appear strong in order to show that you can cope, no matter what is sent your way. Not wanting to appear weak or vulnerable in social situations is inherited from childhood as a coping mechanism. It can mean you sometimes come across as aloof, distant or controlled and you might have difficulty showing vulnerability.

3. The **try hard** driver shows up in you if you believe that life is difficult and struggle is the name of the game. You may have a tendency, especially when stressed, to start too many things but not finish them, believing that there is virtue in trying hard. This is often based on an earlier childhood message that you won't succeed. What's missing is fun, play and being creative.

4. The **please others** driver involves trying to gain affection or approval through working hard and pleasing others. You have a strong need to be liked at all costs. Often triggered by an earlier experience of gaining attention and approval from adults, there's lots of anxiety about others not liking you.

5. The **hurry up** driver means that, to show your worth, you become efficient and

Recognising your drivers

Sometimes the simple awareness of recognising what our main drivers are can be a leap forward, away from the limits the drivers place on us and towards the real potential and possibilities that releasing your drivers makes available to you. Grab your pen and notebook, and go and sit somewhere quiet where you won't be disturbed.

- Start by writing about the driver you most identify with.
- What was the activating event or catalyst for this driver?
- What was it protecting or defending you from?
- How does it show up in your relationships, communication and interactions with others?

- What's the pay-off in holding onto this driver?
- How could you take little steps away from this driver? For example, if you have a 'be perfect' driver, where can you allow some imperfection or messiness in your life or work? Or if you have a 'please others' driver, make a list of three people or situations you could say no to in the next seven days. If you have a 'hurry up' driver, what could you delegate to one of your team and completely let go of? Where could you develop listening more?
- Free write about a time you made a mistake and how it made you feel.

Write now

effective, often working at great speed and taking on more than is necessary. You may have the tendency to overlook the details or important elements of tasks. You're likely to be impatient with others and have high expectations of them, often finishing off tasks for them when your patience runs out.

SEE ALSO

- **WAY 28: Parent, child, adult ego states** (page 88)
- **WAY 29: I'm OK and you're OK** (page 90)

WAY 31 A walk around the Karpman Triangle

'The people in your life don't get in the way of your spiritual practice. They are your spiritual practice.' Shozan Jack Heuber, online quote

How often have you blamed someone else for something that has happened to you? When have you felt bullied or persecuted in some way in your life? Or, when have you found yourself in the opposite position? These are all questions designed to unravel the games people play at a psychological and emotional level.

This is perhaps best captured in the work of Stephen Karpman, a student of Eric Berne, the founder of transactional analysis (TA) (Phillips, 2005). Karpman went on to develop what is commonly known as the Karpman Drama Triangle* (below). Take a minute or two to study the triangle.

Does any of the Karpman Triangle* look familiar? It may help to grab your pen and write down one or two examples of where you've experienced any of the roles.

Now, let's take a look at what each position stands for.

The **victim role** often finds the individual feeling powerless and blaming others for their lack of happiness or success.

The **persecutor role** is often about a win-lose situation in which people are either on the individual's side or against them. In this position, things are seen as black and white, with no room for grey. The persecutor has to be right.

The **rescuer role** operates more from sympathy than genuine empathy. This role sees the rescuer as okay and the person needing rescuing as not okay. Typically, the rescuer believes that the victim is unable to make choices for him or herself.

VICTIM
'I'm blameless'
Safe
'Love me no matter what'

Drama - Crisis
Energy

What's your favourite role?
Consuming

THE KARPMAN DRAMA TRIANGLE

RESCUER
'I'm good'
Accepted

Enabling role - indifference is an important tool

PERSECUTOR
'I'm right'
Power

Your position on the triangle

Reconnect with one of the positions on the Triangle where you recall taking on that particular role.

- Write about the experience for five minutes. What were the feelings, emotions and sensations associated with the role? What was your view of the situation at the time? What glasses were you viewing the experience through at the time? What's your view now?

- Who else was involved in your situation? Can you identify the role they were playing? How did communicating with the two other positions make you feel?

- What was your pay-off for acting from this position on the triangle? What did you not get to do? What did you prevent the other roles from doing? How did your role get in the way of the development and enlightenment of the two other roles?

- Who else was involved in your situation? Can you identify the roles they were playing? Now write about the other two roles in the same way, using the above prompts.

It may not be easy to answer these questions, and this is deliberate. It's easier to see others' faults than it is to see where you can hold yourself responsible. Very often there is huge value in taking time to explore the different roles we play in different situations in our work, relationships and lives. Becoming familiar with the positions on the triangle will give you valuable insight and choices to interrupt your own patterns and behaviours.

Reflections
- What are the emerging patterns and themes from your writing inquiry?
- Which role is your most dominant position?
- Which role did you find it hard to own up to?
- What are the triggers that hook you into these roles?
- How could you change the dynamics of either of the positions?

Rather than spending your time moving around the triangle, use your journal to free write and express your emotions and feelings about the above questions. By doing this, you are bringing greater self-awareness and consciousness to your responses. Ask yourself what responsibility you need to take that will not take you down the path of the victim, the persecutor or the rescuer.

Write now

SEE ALSO

32

Question time

'If I had an hour to solve a problem and my life depended on the solution, I would spend the first 55 minutes determining the proper question to ask, for once I know the proper question, I could solve the problem in less than five minutes.' Albert Einstein (scientist) (Vogt *et al*, 2003)

What's the best question someone ever asked you? I remember my first coaching session, as a 20-year-old. The questions my coach asked caused a stunned silence to descend in the room and I remember thinking I hadn't thought about the questions in that way before. Our best answers don't necessarily emerge from the quality of our thinking, but first and foremost from the quality of the questions we ask ourselves. The right question can lead to creative thought, breakthrough thinking and greater clarity, movement and action.

At the core of a great question is the ability to make you curious and really think outside the box, while at the same time keeping it simple. Some of the world's greatest inventions have come about as a result of the right questions being asked. For example, as a teenager, Einstein asked himself, *'What would the universe look like if I were riding on the end of a light beam at the speed of light?'* (Vogt *et al*, 2003) By using his question as a form of inquiry, Einstein made astonishing advances in the field of science.

In the West, one of the reasons we don't ask better questions is that Western society tends to focus on 'the right answers' rather than discovering the 'right questions'. With such heavy emphasis on knowing the right answer it's not surprising that the answer we're most uncomfortable with is, 'I don't know.' We are afraid of the gap between knowing and not knowing. This feels like unfamiliar territory. It triggers feelings of uncertainty and fear of the unknown. No wonder we become anxious, wanting to escape by spilling out the first answer that comes into our heads. But dare yourself to pause a while. Be open to being in relationship with a question throughout your day and week. Don't push it away. Don't scramble towards the first glimmer of an answer. Sit, breathe, wait, listen and naturally receive. There is a rich, fertile space in that gap in which, when the right tension is allowed to form organically, the better answer or solution will eventually arise.

In a groundbreaking article entitled *Powerful Questions*, Vogt *et al* (2003) list the key qualities of powerful questions, questions which:

- generate curiosity in the listener
- stimulate reflective conversation
- are thought-provoking
- bring underlying assumptions to the surface
- invite creativity and new possibilities
- generate energy and forward movement
- channel attention and focus inquiry
- stay with the participants
- touch a deep meaning
- evoke more questions.

In assessing the results of more than a decade of research and practice in the area of appreciative inquiry*, David Cooperrider stated unequivocally that, *'the most important insight we have learned with Appreciative Inquiry to date is that human systems grow toward what they persistently ask questions* *about*' (Vogt *et al*, 2003), What are your thoughts about that quote? Julio Olalla, founder of the Newfield Network coaching approach, said, '*We are full of answers to questions we never ask*' (Olalla, 2010).

Many questions are not to be answered immediately. In the world of professional coaching, this type of question is referred to as an inquiry question. Once the question is posed, you sit with it over days, weeks, even months. You give yourself permission to grow into the question, to ruminate, to explore. The American African writer Zora Neale Hurston (1973) captured the energy of these questions when she wrote, '*There are years that ask questions and years that answer*'. The message from poet Rainer Maria Rilke is that there is no need to rush to answer: '*Have patience with everything unresolved in your heart. Try to love the questions themselves like locked rooms and like books written in a foreign language* (Rilke, 2000).

SEE ALSO
• **WAY 7: Writing prompts** (page 34)

Tip: Free write some of what has gone through your mind as you've been reading this chapter, in your notebook.

Powerful questions

- Think of a problem or challenge that you have right now. Write a detailed description of the issue in your journal. What help do you need with your issue?

- Look at the list of transformational questions opposite. Print or write them out, cut them into slips and place them in an envelope. Return your focus to your initial problem or challenge.

- Randomly pick a question from the envelope but don't look at it. Free write for five minutes, then take a look at your initial problem and the question you picked from the envelope. Answer the question, and consider whether there is a connection between the two. Place the question back into the envelope, give it a good shake and select again. Don't be surprised if you select the same question more than once. That's a sign that the question has something to reveal to you.

- Repeat this seven times.

- You don't have to have a specific problem to focus on; you could simply pick seven questions as described above and free write your responses.

- It's a great idea to collect powerful questions as you notice them being asked.

Transformational questions

What would happen if I did nothing at all?	What would be a brave thing for me to do right now?	What would be the craziest thing for me to do right now?	What would my more logical, rational side suggest I do?
The question I really don't want to ask is...	If I knew my life depended on it, what would happen next?	What am I most uncomfortable about right now?	The question I really don't want to answer is...
What stands between me and resolving this issue?	What am I not saying or wanting to admit right now?	What am I avoiding right now?	If I was looking at this challenge upside down, what would be different?
Who could help me with this issue right now?	Draw a picture quickly that describes how you're feeling about the issue.	What questions would I like to pose to your challenge?	What strengths do I have that will help you with this issue right now?
Think of someone you admire. What advice would they give you about handling your challenge?	What if I did have the potential right now to resolve this issue? What would my first action be? Then what?	On a scale of 1–10, with 1 being the worst it has ever been and 10 being the issue resolved, where are you right now on the scale?	What's the smallest thing I could do in the next 60 minutes to change how I'm feeling about this challenge?
If I had a magic wand, what would I wish for?	What have I survived in the past that would help me now?	If I could turn the clock back 24 hours, what would I do differently?	What secret super powers could I pull out of the bag to support me right now?
What opportunities are there?	What does my intuition tell me to do?	If I knew there was no way I could fail, what would I do next?	What's the pay-off for holding on to this challenge?
My greatest heroine or hero would advise me to...	My inner child would advise me to...	My 100-year-old self would advise me to...	My inner wise self would advise me to...

1 2 3 4 5 6 7 8
9 10 11 12 13 14
15 16 17 18 19
20 21 22 23 24
25 26 27 28 29
30 31 32 **33 34**
35 36 37 38 39
40 41 42 43 44
45 46 47 48 49

Chapter 5

WRITING THERAPY: CHANGE THE SCRIPT!

How often have you felt, 'If I could only change my life story'? Well now you can, by applying some of the techniques and approaches of narrative therapists Michael White and David Epston. Much of the content of this chapter has been inspired by the real possibilities that narrative therapy* offers you to re-author your life story. By engaging in the 'Write now' practices in this chapter you will learn how to re-author and reframe your own life experiences on the page. Rather than settle for 'This happened to me', you will learn how to reframe and rewrite your story to give it your own meaning.

This chapter shows how fiction writing can create a 'safe enough' distance between you and your life experiences to allow you to achieve a different and useful perspective on your own life story. We take a look at forgiveness and how writing about forgiveness brings its own healing and benefits, how to make best use of your perceived failures and how to transform them on the page. The chapter ends by considering how writing can help you to 'unpack' your personal history and your relationship with money, on the page.

WAY 33 Rewrite your life script

'A person of substance always has a past.'
Fiona Harold (life coach)
(www.fionaharold.com)

What if you had the power to write yourself a new life story? Whilst you can't delete the narrative of your past, you can redefine it and rewrite your future life script*. According to the work of narrative therapists Michael White and David Epston, this therapeutic approach is not only possible but really works. Working with the principles of narrative therapy* can be a powerful way of rewriting and re-authoring many of your life stories, giving them new perspectives and defining them in more empowering and liberating ways.

Here, you'll learn how to self-apply straightforward tools and techniques that narrative therapists use in collaboration with their clients. But this in no way overlooks the fact that the work of narrative therapy is complex and takes time, with therapist and client working in collaboration.

Because of the possibility that you might get in touch with painful memories from your past, please ensure beforehand that you have a close friend or family member you can confide in. If your feelings become too difficult to manage, please consult a mental health practitioner or therapist who can provide you with the necessary support and guidance.

So, just how do you begin the journey of re-authoring your life stories? First of all,

I suggest starting small. Think of an event from your life you'd like to work with. The key is to return to the event and look at it from a number of different perspectives. For example, Wendy's childhood had a series of traumatic events, which shaped the stories she told herself about her life. But through her work with various therapists she safely revisited the scenes of her past and rediscovered pieces of her story that were affirming and empowering, which had been overlooked or dismissed.

Narrative therapist Kristy Schubert (2007) refers to 'sparkling moments' – those little or big occasions where you have acted on some deep hope or in accordance with some deep value. If those moments aren't included in the explanations of you that have been repeated over and over again, you wave your hand at them and say, 'Oh, that really doesn't show who I am. It's just an exception.' These moments have not been written into your explanation or account of your life stories so they get overlooked, discounted and sometimes completely forgotten about.

Employing a curious mind and respectful stance helps when engaged in this work. Being curious will enable you to go beyond the stories you've told yourself, to see what else lies there in your landscape of stories. So, how is this done? In her book *What is Narrative Therapy*? narrative therapist Alice Morgan (2000) suggests identifying alternative stories that do not support or sustain problems but rather create new possibilities and assist you rather than hold you back. The power is in your hands to re-author new and preferred stories for your life and your relationships.

Giving your story new meaning

- Select a story or period from your past that you would like to re-author.

- Set a timer for 30 minutes. Write your memory of the event in longhand in your journal or notebook.

- Normally, a narrative therapist would talk through the event with you to uncover missed or overlooked actions that were empowering and affirming. Imagine you are doing the same thing. Read through your description, holding in mind the question, 'What might I have forgotten or overlooked about my actions and my behaviours at the time?'

- For example, your parents' divorce may have been painful for you as a 12-year-old. But have you overlooked the great relationship you had as a result with your school friend, with whom you're still in touch? Where would this new storyline go? What new adventures could you create on the page? Where and how would the storyline link into other events in your life?

When Wendy asked herself about the event from childhood she was re-authoring, she discovered how brave she had been. She had forgotten how she had found her voice at the time and spoken out. Yet for years she had overlooked this rich detail, preferring instead to go along with the story of being a victim. Narrative therapists refer to this as 'externalising'. Discovering this also led Wendy to recognise other places in her life where she had the courage to speak up. Suddenly, this life event had new meaning as the alternative story.

To add further empowerment to your story, try one of the following:
- Give yourself the persona of a hero or heroine and tell your life event from that place.
- Give yourself superpowers based on your strengths, and over-amplify them.
- Imagine reading your new story aloud to a cherished daughter, son, grandchild or godchild, with you at the centre of the story as the hero or heroine.
- Write a letter to one of the characters involved in the life event you are re-authoring, letting them know how you feel and what you now stand for or what you would have done differently

Don't underestimate the energy required for this psychological and emotional work. Build in small treats and rewards after working with the issues in this chapter, especially.

Write now

SEE ALSO

WAY 34 Fact or fiction

'I write fiction mostly to try to make sense of my own petty and profound misery, and I fail every time; but every time, I come away with a particular state of contentment as if it was just the trying that mattered.'
Chris Adrian, 2007 (paediatrician and novelist)

If you ask most fiction writers and novelists what is the most common question they're asked by readers, they will without hesitation reply, '*How much of your story is actually based on true life?*'. Their responses are interesting, ranging from '*None of it*' to '*Well, there are traces of my own life that I have tweaked and changed, but my own experiences have helped me give voice and meaning to the subject I'm writing about*'.

The truth is that for many fiction writers their own lived experiences will have been the catalyst for many of the imagined stories and characters that appear on the page. After all, as Salmon Rushdie is quoted in *A Writer's Book of Days* (Reeves, 1999) as saying, '*I've always been a writer who has written from some place reasonably close to experiences, but it's always used, turned into something, put somewhere else, made something of.*'

So, just how can you take your painful experiences and escape the psychological tangles that often emerge from the secrets and lies of your own past? One way is to disguise the real person who was part of your life story as someone else. That's what many fiction writers do. Your mother, who was married for many years, becomes a character who is single and of a different race and culture, making her almost unrecognisable on the page.

Yet the emotions, the raw feelings you had of your mother as you were growing up, become embedded as part of your new character's experience, making her feel real and authentic.

Take novelist Natasha Simpson, who writes '*In one book, I wrote about a savage rape, a subject that has always interested me. It's about power as much as sex, and my mother had a huge and terrifying power with her rages and abuse... My latest novel contains much that is a way of exploring stuff about my mother. I never wanted to write directly about her, but my writing gave me enough insight that I'm now much more peaceful about her*' (Neustatter, 2012).

There will be times when writing about people, events or experiences in your life will render them too terrifying. Taking a step back, writing in the third person or changing the identity and location of your character can give you the freedom to delve into your material without the fear of it consuming you with pain or overwhelming memories. Janet Fitch, author of the novel *White Oleander*, says, '*I use my fiction to explore my own unconscious issues. I usually don't even know what's going on with me until I'm writing*' (Fitch, 2006)

In her book *The Writer's Portable Therapist*, psychotherapist Rachel Ballon (2007) tells writers, '*Please don't write directly about your latest family feud or your broken love affair. No, that would be boring to everyone. What you need to learn, in order to be creative as a writer, is to take an aspect of your life that is an emotional experience and transform it into fiction.*' I agree to a certain extent with Ballon but would add that your journal or notebook is a safe and private space for you to write freely about that latest family feud knowing that it is for your eyes only.

A new twist

Think about an emotional experience from your life that was perhaps a difficult challenge for you. Now give the characters involved new identities. You might make them a different age, height, colour, gender or race. Next, think about the location: what will be different in your new story? Describe the location in detail. Now, write about the experience, keeping all the emotional details intact but writing in the new characters, identities and location that give your story a brand new twist.

Write now

SEE ALSO

- **WAY 7: Writing prompts** (page 34)
- **WAY 8: Visual writing prompts** (page 39)

WAY 35 Forgiveness (part 1)

'There is no love without forgiveness, and there is no forgiveness without love.'
Bryant H McGill, 2012 (editor and author)

Your journal is a place of sanctuary and forgiveness. It will forgive you for everything and anything you feel ashamed of or bad about. Your journal will not judge your indiscretions, your poor decisions or your missed opportunities. Neither will it berate you (even though you may feel you have a right to do that). With its still, calm presence and its understanding, compassionate heart, it will hold it all in and offer you forgiveness.

Over the years I have read and written a fair bit on the subject of forgiveness but life and its experiences have taught me that true forgiveness emanates from the heart and not from the head. We also need to sit with our vulnerabilities, which often opens us up to the feelings of shame and other emotions that we try hard to not feel. Forgiveness requires going deep into this work. You may find researcher Brené Brown's (2010) work on vulnerability and shame really helpful. Let's acknowledge together that we don't take this work lightly. I invite you to enter this space and write from your heart and not from your head.

So let's get to work. Get yourself comfortable and find a new page in your notebook or journal. Take it slow and gentle. There's no rush with this sacred work. Take a moment to bring to mind an occasion in your life where you did something that on reflection you would like to ask forgiveness for. You can go as far back as you wish. You can choose an incident from childhood or an experience that's more recent.

Set a timer for 20 minutes. Begin with the alternate nostril breathing practice outlined in **WAY 10: Stilling the mind to write** (page 42) to centre yourself. Free write, describing the experience in as much detail as you can. Stop when the 20 minutes is up. Take a few minutes to sit quietly before you move on.

Well done for writing down this experience or event. Reflect on your writing so far. How does it feel getting it out on paper? What have you let go of? How has this made you feel? What has it freed you up to be able to do or be?

It's worth taking time out to think about the invisible hold that forgiveness can have over you. For example, if you still have feelings about your contribution to the event, it's likely that you are still energetically linked to the past, the person or the experience.

Then there's the impact of how you feel about the event and how this influences the way you think about yourself. It's quite likely that what you think or say to yourself won't be self-affirming or positive.

The past is what it is, and to forgive is to give up the possibility of a better past.

SEE ALSO
- **WAY 23: A paper ritual for releasing your emotions** (page 76)
- **WAY 36: Forgiveness (part 2)** (page 108)
- **WAY 47: Gratitude journal** (page 136)

Focused writing

Research by Dr James Pennebaker, psychology professor at the University of Texas at Austin (1997) has shown that short-term, focused writing does have an impact on how people feel. Other research by Pennebaker (1997) and others shows that writing about emotional trauma leads to improved health and well-being.

Here's the original assignment given to those taking part in Pennebaker's research:

'Over the next four days, write about your deepest emotions and thoughts about the emotional upheaval that has been influencing your life the most. In your writing really let go and explore the event and how it has affected you. You might tie this experience to your childhood, your relationship with your parents, people you have loved or love now or even your career. Write continuously for 20 minutes and then stop.'

The key guidance was to write for 20 minutes only, for four consecutive days. You are invited to try this writing practice for the next four days, about an emotional upheaval that has been influencing your own life. Once you have completed the four days, return to this page and read on.

Welcome back. How did it go? Have you recorded your thoughts and your reflections based on your four days of writing? If not, do so now.

The findings from Pennebaker's (1997) research concluded that writing about the event in a focused and concentrated way helped individuals to organise the experience and make meaning of it. Many reported that they had a better understanding of the experience. Noted health benefits included improved sleep patterns, improved social connections and fewer visits to the doctor.

Writing about a trauma or difficult time can help to put the experience in context and allow you to have a different perspective on the experience itself. To complete this work, take a blank sheet of paper and write a letter or list outlining any regrets or disappointments you have from your past. Take your time with this writing practice. When you have finished, place your letter in an envelope and seal it. Research (Bolton, 2011) has found that *'descriptions of regretted decisions, sealed thus, decreased negative feelings about the decision'*. Post your letter to a fictional address or perform a burning ritual, as in **WAY 23: A paper ritual for releasing your emotion**s (page 76).

Time now for a nurturing treat – or give yourself some quality alone time.

Write now

WAY 36 Forgiveness (part 2)

'If we survive childhood we have enough material to last a lifetime.'
Flannery O'Connor, 2007 (writer)

Forgiveness is sometimes referred to as 'the spiritual laxative'. In many ways and on many levels it is just that; when you really forgive, much is released and discarded in terms of toxic feelings, pain and emotions.

When journaling and free writing about your painful emotions, what makes the difference is the way in which you write about how you feel. Studies by James Pennebaker (1997) revealed that the more people described positive emotions while writing, the more likely they were to be healthier afterwards. But when it came to describing and writing about negative emotions, the opposite was true and poorer health conditions were reported.

Together with Pennebaker, University of Texas graduate student Martha Francis developed a text analysis software program called Linguistic Inquiry and Word Count (LIWC), which evaluates the frequency of word usage in writing samples (Connor, 2008). Francis's research showed that:

- words like happy, love or good were used often
- negative words like hurt, ugly or angry were used, but in moderation
- writers who were more reflexive, who showed insight and who communicated through the use of words like 'understand', 'realise' or 'know', had the greatest benefits

- over time, the writing samples changed from disjointed narratives to coherent stories with a beginning, middle and end.

There is little value in denying the difficult feelings you may have about someone or an event from your life but, as you write, it can act as a conduit to transforming your emotions and feelings and guiding them towards a forgiving heart and, ultimately, a peaceful and graceful resolution. As social scientist Katheryn Rhoads Meek highlights in a research paper, *The Science Of Forgiveness* (2001), studies confirm that the practice of forgiveness is directly related to emotional healing and the building of peaceful communities.

You may well have a range of views about the meaning of the word 'forgiveness'. Take a minute right now and jot down your first thoughts on the following:
- My definition of forgiveness is...
- What is forgiveness not?

As Dr. Stephen Post and Jill Neimark say in *Why Good Things Happen to Good People* (2008): '*In order to forgive you must tell the true story of exactly what happened, grieve it fully, and then turn away from grudges, bitterness, and the kind of ruminating that amplifies the story and gives it too much replay time.*'

SEE ALSO
- **WAY 35: Forgiveness (part 1)** (page 106)
- **WAY 47: Gratitude journal** (page 136)

Hidden blessings

Ernest Hemingway (1929) wrote, '*many of us are broken but we are stronger at the broken places*'.

- Write about the hidden blessings in three of your most difficult life challenges.

- Write a letter to yourself from your inner wise writing self, which reminds you of all your wonderful qualities and why forgiving others and yourself will set you free.

- Choose a ritual that you will perform to mark this stage of your writing journey. You might want to blow out a candle, say a prayer, read aloud a poem or release a balloon to symbolise letting go.

When you have finished this practice, it's time to celebrate. I want you to stop and do something kind and nurturing for yourself, something that will take care of your emotions and feelings.

Write now

WAY 37 The F Word

'And the day came when the risk it took to remain tightly closed in a bud was more painful than the risk it took to blossom.'
Anais Nin, 1944–47 (Diarist)

What if failure is the beginning of your story and not the end? We don't talk about failure enough. It's a taboo subject at dinner conversations, skirted around in work environments, pushed to the back of your own mind. The lack of conversation about failure causes the individual to create stories about other people's lives and other people's lack of failure. So as this book is about writing, let's take a look at some of the failures writers have lived through in terms of rejected book proposals.

- Clarissa Pinkola Estes took 20 years to write *Women Who Run With The Wolves* and then faced rejection 47 times (McMeekin, 2000). It became a best seller.

- L Frank Baum, who penned the *Wizard of Oz*, had the book rejected a mere 40 times (Pickard & Lott, 2003). It became one of the best-known films of all time.

- The film *We Need To Talk About Kevin* was based on a book by Lionel Shriver that was rejected by 30 publishers. Even her agent didn't like it (Butler-Bowden, 2012). She eventually won the Orange Prize for Fiction for the book in 2005. It was her seventh book and she had toiled for two decades without recognition. Imagine if she had given up?

What's your interpretation of failure? Are you one step closer to your goal or one step further away? Is your glass half full or half empty?

Before you read on, free write your thoughts and responses to the following questions, which will help you get a different perspective on perceived failures:

- If I floated above my failure and looked down on the scene from a different angle, what would I see?

- If I was an objective observer, what would I be seeing?

- Imagine yourself interviewing the failure. Ask things like: *What's the purpose of your visit? How long will you be around? What are your strengths? What are the messages you want to deliver? How can I reclaim my power from your perceived threat? How long do you intend to be around? What scares you most?* The purpose of this is to explore the motive or tactic of the failure as a problem or challenge, whilst giving you the power through your questioning to reclaim your power.

Failure shows up in your life with the intention of directing you towards a different route in life. This is unlikely to be the route that you have chosen but when we explore the outcomes of failure, it is rarely as bad as it seems.

Failure shapes you and makes you who you will become. It is the training ground of resilience, humility and spiritual awakening. It gives you the humane factor and very often wakes you up to life.

'The nevers'

Part of transforming the energy of the word 'failure' is accepting and embracing what the existential psychologist James Bugental calls 'the nevers' (Bridges, 2004). Accepting 'the nevers' brings home the reality that there are many things in life we will never be.

I guess that I'm never going to be the head of the firm... never going to have children of my own... never going to be a great writer... never going to be rich... never going to be famous' (Bridges, 2004).

Taking your time, get down on the page all the things you want to acknowledge that never worked out and all the things that will never be. Time to set it down on the page once and for all. Lists are good way of getting 'the nevers' out and releasing them onto the page.

Take a long hard look at your 'nevers'. Perhaps there is some grieving to do at the realisation of what will not be. Or perhaps setting them down to rest on the page has created space for new possibilities to emerge. Right now, be gentle with yourself. Give yourself a long, lingering hug, or ask for a hug from a loved one.

Tip: Marianne Williamson, spiritual teacher and author, wrote that after every devastating loss comes a stunning win (Williamson, 1994). Take a moment to consider examples from your own life of losses that were eventually transformed into stunning wins. Make a note of these in your journal or notebook. It's good to have that written evidence to look back on when we are in the grip of challenge and change and have forgotten what could be waiting for us on the other side.

Writing about your failures, whether current or in the past, can help you on a number of levels. It connects you to those muscles, those parts of your strengths and skills that you may have neglected using. There is medicine waiting to be retrieved in your failure narratives. Sometimes the failure is for a good reason. A failed relationship releases you to meet the love of your life. A job in a company that that goes under gives you licence to do what you

love. In previous 'Ways' you learned about the benefits of writing about traumatic events. This Way focuses on getting your failure stories out onto the blank page.

SEE ALSO
- **WAY 9: Inner Wise Writing Self** (page 40)
- **WAY 35: Forgiveness (part 1)** (page 106)
- **WAY 36: Forgiveness (part 2)** (page 108)
- **WAY 47: Gratitude journal** (page 136)

38 Money, money, money

> *'There is no better way to earn money than to do the things that you love to do. Money can flow into your experience through endless avenues. It is not the choice of the craft that limits the money that flows, but only your attitude toward money.'*
> Esther and Jerry Hicks (metaphysical teachers) (www.abraham-hicks.co.uk)

Many of us have a complicated relationship with money. It symbolises our identification with our self-worth and self-esteem and how we are viewed by ourselves and others. Your relationship with money may also have a complicated story of your own family history, fortunes and misfortunes. Money is story. Writing about your relationship with money can be an important step to changing your relational dynamics with money and your relationship with it. The truth about your relationship with money is not just about your finances or the number; it's about emotions and experiences.

One way of writing about money in order to better understand your relationship with it is to identify on the page your personal money story and the script you may have inherited as a result. Just as with narrative therapy, you have the power of the pen and the ability to rewrite your own money scripts. A recent report by Kiplinger states, *'when misguided money beliefs stem from childhood trauma or are laden with emotion, the combination is especially toxic'* (McCarthy, 2012). These money scripts formed in childhood subconsciously drive your behaviours and actions.

For years I was aware of my own personal money history and how this informed the money script I had embedded. I grew up in a working class family in south London and my dad worked hard as a builder and carpenter. Very early on I internalised that to earn money, you had to work very hard, not take holidays, do extra work on the side and so on. This was complicated by the fact that I had low self-esteem and lots of self-doubt as I was growing up so that by the time I reached university I used spending money to cover up how empty and alone I was feeling.

Brad Klontz, a clinical psychologist, suggests that our money scripts fall broadly into four categories (Kiplinger, 2012):

1. Money avoidance – avoiding or ignoring your money issues, which can show up in over-spending or under-spending

2. Money worship – investing in the belief that money can buy you happiness

3. Money status – basing your value on your financial worth

4. Money vigilance – being the one who is always saving for a rainy day; helpful to a certain extent but it can result in a lack of spending on oneself, leading to a lack of enjoyment in the present moment

Which category would you say your relationship with money falls into? Many of our money scripts can be traced back to our early relationships within our family systems, and these scripts become our drivers. When I was writing my first book I uncovered a family story I'd had no idea about, which added further fuel to my own money story. I discovered that,

Your relationship with money

What's your earliest memory of money? Write down your story. What messages did you take from this memory? How has it helped you? How has it hindered you?

- What was your father's relationship with money? What was your mother's relationship with money?

- What money beliefs did you inherit while you were growing up?

- Use the ABCDE model in **WAY 25: Challenge your beliefs** (page 82) to get a handle on your money beliefs.

- Dispute your negative beliefs about money. Which parts of the beliefs are true? Which are untrue?

- Quick-think new and creative ways of approaching your relationship with money.

- Create a money memories timeline. Draw a timeline in your notebook or journal, starting from childhood and showing your significant money moments to date. Make a note of recurring themes and patterns along your timeline.

- When have you had a healthy relationship with money, and how are you when this happens? Make a note of specific times and examples from your past. What are your healthy money habits, no matter how small? List as many as you can think of. How can you build on these habits?

- What would you love to do, even if you weren't paid to do it?

Write now

while working on the Panama Canal in the early 1900s, my grandfather won the lottery, returned to Barbados a rich man, spent the lot and ended up a pauper. Instantly, I began making connections not only with my own money scripts but also with the money scripts of both my parents. My money scripts had me swinging between conflicting messages about money – working hard for it then spending it once you'd accumulated it – which haunted me for much of my teenage years and young adulthood. Your journal is an ideal place to explore your money relationships on the page. Use your writing to identify the patterns and challenges with your own relationship with money.

SEE ALSO
- **WAY 33: Rewrite your life script** (page 102)
- **WAY 34: Fact or fiction** (page 104)
- **WAY 39: Rewrite your money scripts** (page 114)

WAY 39

Rewrite your money scripts

'It turns out that when money is the topic, most of us need permission to talk about it because we've been taught it's not a suitable topic of conversation.' L Perle, 2006

The way you use and think about money can have a powerful impact on your well-being. It can be very difficult to change long-established ways of dealing with and discussing your finances. Your journal can be a very effective tool in rewriting your 'money script'. You can learn how to transform your relationship with money by studying its energy and how you relate to it. The first step in rewriting your script is identifying the patterns and themes of your relationship with money.

SEE ALSO
- **WAY 33: Rewrite your life script** (page 102)
- **WAY 38: Money, money, money** (page 112)

Keeping a money diary

To help you slow down on your spending, buy yourself a small, pocket-sized notebook. This is your money diary. Every day for the next seven days, make a note of what you spend, and what else is happening in your life when you do so.

When the week is up, find a quiet space in your day when you won't be disturbed. You will be using the time to examine your patterns of spending. Have a look through your recordings. What do you notice? What are the themes and patterns? Where and when do you have a tendency to overspend? What happens just before you overspend? What could you do instead? Take your exploration further by considering what has been going on in your life when you've found yourself struggling with money. What are your normal, everyday emotional responses to money?

Keeping a written record of your financial responses can create a gap between the beliefs that drive your actions and behaviours around money.

Compare and contrast the money themes that are emerging from your money memories timeline from **WAY 38: Money, money, money** (page 112) and your money diary. What are you noticing?

Next turn your focus to your money scripts that you identified in **WAY 38**. Take your time and work through the following questions in your journal or notebook:

- Which of your money scripts feels very emotive?
- What's true about your money scripts?
- What's false or distorted about your money scripts?
- What can be re-edited or reframed about your money scripts?

1 2 3 4 5 6 7 8
9 10 11 12 13 14
15 16 17 18 19
20 21 22 23 24
25 26 27 28 29
30 31 32 33 34
35 36 37 38 39
40 41 42 43 44
45 46 47 48 49

Chapter 6

NATURE WISDOM, BODY WISDOM AND WRITING WISDOM

Nature has always been an inspiration for writers and this chapter opens up a space for you to explore your own relationship with nature, as a writer. It highlights the very important connection between nature and writing. Research and studies repeatedly confirm the many health and psychological benefits of being with nature. With this in mind, the idea of walking is explored and reveals how walking as a practice is a valuable activity for deepening our well-being and practice as writers. And there's nothing like a bit of poetry to ground you in nature and walking so we explore the value of poetry and how to use it for therapeutic purposes. We then move in to explore the body through the senses, along with exploring the psychological and health benefits of starting a 'gratitude journal' and cultivating a 'gratitude practice'. The final 'ways' aim to rekindle the almost lost art of personal letter writing by encouraging you to write letters to your younger and older selves. The chapter closes with a ritual to bring your writing journey to a place of genuine acknowledgement and appreciation.

WAY 40 Writing with nature

'Nature is something within which we flourish, so having it be more a part of our lives is critical, specially when we live and work in built environments.'
Richard M Ryan, 2010 (Professor of Psychology at the University of Rochester)

Nature is a source of energy and inspiration for your writing. What's the weather like today? Take your notebook and pen and write a description of the weather outside your window. What colour is the sky? What smells can you pick up? What sounds are in the air? If you are outside, touch a plant or something belonging to the earth. What's the texture like? Nature is an abundant inspiration for your writing in many ways. There are huge benefits from getting out and writing in nature and there is so much you can gain from the rich connection with Mother Earth that can influence what you write and be easily transferred to the page.

There are many reasons why nature can be a source of inspiration for your writing. Nature restores balance and reconnects you with your true nature. When you feel your writing putting you in touch with deep emotions, allow nature to be a grounding and calming presence. You can do this by getting outside and simply standing or lying on the earth – let Mother Earth embrace and hold you for a few minutes. There are plenty of ways to do this without drawing attention to yourself: standing with your back against a tree, or sitting on the grass, a low, sturdy tree branch, a large rock or a park bench. Always carry your notebook or journal with you.

A report published in *Science Daily* (2010) showed that spending time in nature makes people feel more alive. To establish whether the feeling of being more alive was the result of physical activity or social mixing, five further studies were conducted involving 537 college students. In the first experiment, students were led on a 15-minute walk through indoor hallways or along a tree-lined path. In the second, they viewed photographic scenes of buildings and landscapes. In the third experiment, students imagined themselves in a variety of situations, active and sedentary, inside and out, with and without others. The two final experiments tracked students' moods and energy levels throughout the day using diary entries; over four days or two weeks, students recorded their exercise, social interactions, time spent outside and exposure to the natural environment. Across all methodologies, students felt consistently more energetic when they spent time in natural settings or imagined themselves in such situations.

Just as people in hospital recover more quickly when they can see a tree from the window, you can top up your falling energy levels and flailing spirits by immersing yourself in nature. Nature is by far our quickest route to reconnecting with the senses. The smell of fallen bark or the scent of jasmine flowers from a hedgerow or a flowering rosebush can be intoxicating. By using nature to awaken the senses, you can bring your writing alive on the page.

Nature's beauty and originality provides thousands of writing prompts for your writing. Whether it's examining the complex design and patterns of tree bark, the colour of a stream or the different shades of the sky, nature provides

a constant stream from which we can extract ideas and content for our writing. Connecting with the rhythms of nature and following her seasons draws parallels with the cycles of our own lives. Nature is a reflecting mirror, a reverent and resourceful teacher. We can learn much from her, both on and off the page.

SEE ALSO
- **WAY 41: Conversations with trees** (page 122)
- **WAY 42: Walking and writing** (page 126)

Tip: Here are a couple of questions to mull over in your mind and then onto the page:

- Who would you be and how would your life be different if you spent as much time in nature as you did in front of the computer or TV screen?

- What would be different about your life if you spent more time in nature?

Wish you were here!

When you were young, do you remember the ritual of going on holiday and feeling compelled to buy picture postcards with scenes of your holiday destination? Did you sit down religiously and write a range of messages from '*I'm okay, Mum and Dad,*' to the censored codes to a girlfriend about a holiday romance?

Today, try reviving the tradition of sending a holiday postcard but with a slight twist. Your postcard will be sent from a real or imagined place in nature.

In the 'postcard' provided opposite, write a descriptive message to a loved one or friend, describing your favourite place in nature. Where is your place? Bring it alive by describing the sounds, the smells, the textures and how you feel in the space.

Perhaps it is the pungent smell of the sea or the mossy scents of the woods that brings you alive. Get really specific. What colours are the plants? Describe them, imagining that your reader is colour-blind. Tune into the weather, capture it in words, images or metaphors. And sign off with '*Wish you were here!*'

It is easy to walk through the weather and not notice its different forces and elements. We become immune to the real life force of the natural world and sooner or later this spreads into an immunity from our interior world. Nature wakes us up to the external, which in turn puts us back in touch with the internal.

Write now

Conversations with trees

'I frequently tramped eight or ten miles through the deepest snow to keep an appointment with a Beech tree, or a yellow Birch or an old acquaintance among the pines.' Henry David Thoreau (novelist) (George, 2011)

I love trees, I always have done. My admiration for them has grown deeper over the years. In *The Secret Life of Trees*, Colin Tudge (2005) writes, *'The only proper attitude towards them is one of gratitude, because we really do rely on them for our own existence; and of reverence, because they are really wondrous, and, in the end, however excellent our science may become, they are beyond our ken. I am sure that is how most people, in their bones, feel towards trees.'* How do you feel in your bones about trees?

Being in the company of trees has many therapeutic benefits. Just being around them reduces stress and lowers blood pressure, and spending time in woods and forests has a calming effect. Trees have always been writers' friends and you will gain much from taking your writing outside and seeking the company of trees on your writing journey.

Native Americans refer to trees as The Standing People and believe that trees inherit the spirits of their ancestors. Trees are nature's storytellers. Think of a tree and you will think of a story. Once, when discussing my shock at the cutting down of a beautiful tamarind tree that once lived feet from my mothers house in Barbados, she simply blurted out, *'That tree have enough secrets'*. I guess she was talking about all the secrets and conversations the tree had been privy to over the years. Perhaps that is why we love to sit by trees or rest our back against a huge tree-trunk or find a spot under her shade to sit and rest.

> Tip: What is your earliest childhood memory of a tree? Where was it? Describe it in as much detail as you can.

In his stunning book, *Bark*, Cedric Pollet (2010) encourages you to really see trees: *'So open your eyes and take the time to look: the trees will be happy to unveil their secrets to you.'*

Today, I want you to make a date when you will go and spend time with a tree. When you are on your tree date, rather than study your tree from afar I'd like to encourage you to get up close and intimate and study its bark. Pollet describes Bark as *'a complex structure that evolves constantly over time. Its inner part is made up of living cells that form the conducting vessels for the sap that travels down the leaves to all the organs of the tree. The outer layer, made up of dead cells, forms a protective barrier against the onslaught of the outside world'* (Pollet, 2010). Can you see any relationship between you as a human being and trees?

Spending time with trees has a number of benefits for your writing and your healing. Because they are calming and grounding, they are great to write beside. By really noticing trees, you increase your observational skills and this in turn opens up your descriptive language on the page.

In *A Writer's Book of Days*, Judy Reeves (1999) quotes Henry David Thoreau: '*Pause when you will to examine the intricacies of a tree, its branches stretching up and out, the veins of a leaf, the tracks of a creature. No need for conversation. Better to walk in silence to notice and observe. Listen to the symphony of the place, the play of sand against sand.*

Let the geometrics of light lead you deeper into the woods and the trail that you follow will be the one's less travelled.'

SEE ALSO
- **WAY 40: Writing with nature** (page 118)
- **WAY 42: Walking and writing** (page 126)

Bark

This practice invites you to spend time drinking in the bark of a tree through your eyes and sense of touch, using the visual writing prompt of tree bark.

If you can't get to a tree, use the visual writing prompt here instead. Take a few minutes and write about what you see in this tree's bark. Describe the colours; imagine touching it. How would it feel against the skin of your fingertips? How many colours do you see in this image? If you knew the story of this tree, what would it be?

If you are out in nature and you have a camera on your mobile phone, choose your tree and take several close-up photographs of its bark. Sit and examine the images and write about what you see and feel. Touch the bark and write about the sensations you experience. Use the prompts in the previous paragraph in the same way.

End by free writing a story about a particular memory or relationship with a tree from the past.

Write now

Tip: Each tree species carries its own wisdom and healing qualities. Spend time with an oak tree, whose healing properties will strengthen individuals whose life force has been strained and unbalanced. Being in the presence of a beech tree (known as the Mother of the Woods) can apparently help you to let go of fixed ideas and opinions that are holding you back. You can find much more on the healing and wisdom of trees in the wonderful book *Tree Wisdom: The definitive guidebook to the myth, folklore and healing power of trees* by Jacqueline Memory Paterson (1996), one of my all time favourite tree books.

WAY 42 Walking and writing

'On days when I walk, my day unfolds with powerful synchronicity. I have talked not just with God, but with both sides of myself. Perhaps most important, the land has talked to me. I love the clarity the flow such walking brings to me.'
Julia Cameron, 1996 (writer)

Walking and writing go hand in hand. Many writers have written deeply and passionately about the benefits that walking brings to them and their writing practice. Julia Cameron, author of more than 20 non-fiction books on writing and creativity, writes constantly in her work about the virtues of walking: '*When we are too heady, too full of chatter and clatter of our stress filled lives, our spiritual energy returns to us through our feet*' (Cameron, 1982). Many writers talk of the connection that walking brings between themselves and the earth. William Blake walked regularly along the trails of the haymakers from central London to Peckham Rye to visit friends. Charles Dickens was a committed walker, often walking through the early hours of the night. And it was reported that Beethoven would stride around the city of Vienna in all weathers, dreaming up symphonies and ignoring everyone who greeted him.

In a car or a train you are disconnected but walking is a symphony for your senses. Cameron believes that when we walk we are tuning in and listening to our interior lives. We open the floodgates to listening to ourselves on a high level frequency (known as the alpha state* of being). Walking also carries multiple health benefits. Recent research indicates that walking can halve the risk of stroke and heart disease, reduce breast cancer by up to 40 per cent and decrease the risk of type 2 diabetes (*Good Housekeeping*, 2008).

Walking can significantly contribute to your writing. It is a way to get out of your head and into the present. A good walk can unclutter your brain, empty a busy mind and unravel your thoughts and ideas. Get outside into nature and walk for at least 30 minutes as often as you can. If time presents a challenge, consider getting off the bus two stops early and walking to work. Decide what day of the week will be your walking day.

In an article in *The Guardian* (2010), writers were asked to describe their relationship with walking. Joan Bakewell, journalist and broadcaster wrote, '*the city life itself cuts you off from the seasons, but walking restores your awareness*'. I can't say I totally agree with the comments about city life but our modern-day lives do disconnect and dull the senses and walking is a sure way of bringing the senses alive. Former poet laureate Andrew Motion comments in the same feature, '*walking gives you ideas, unblocks blockages and sets up rhythms in our head*'.

Your weekly walk can be used to switch over from the over-relied on left brain to the wider terrain of the right brain. With the left brain at ease, the right brain is free to roam and make subconscious connections. Walk to work your way through problems and find your way to solutions. You will open yourself to a deeper engagement with the sensual world.

A mindful walk

Buddhists practice *kinhin*, which is a slow, purposeful mindful walking meditation, connected to the breath. Over the next 24 hours, plan a 20-minute mindful walk outside with your camera. As you walk mindfully, focus on the colours you encounter. Don't just see green. Ask yourself what shade of green it is. Study the textures and designs of the buildings around you. Look up. What do you see? What colour is the sky today? How many colours can you see? Invent a new range of colours as you walk. Take photos of whatever captures your attention. Take photos from different levels, above and below, different angles or upside down. Have fun, play and really see. Return to your notebook and write about your adventure with the outside world. Use the images you have taken as visual writing prompts for today and future writing days.

Write now

Be sure to walk with your notebook or writing paper tucked into your pocket or bag. You never know what scenes you will come across, what conversations you might overhear, what ideas might spring to mind. If you're feeling stuck on the page, down your tools and get out into nature or your local neighbourhood and walk. As you walk, refrain from using your mobile phone. Heed the warning from David Hockney, artist and writer, who said that speaking on your cell phone is, '*wasting your time, because you may look but not really see*' (Johnson, 2010).

A weekly walk replenishes the senses. It's a must for your weekly schedule.

SEE ALSO
- **WAY 40: Writing with nature** (page 118)
- **WAY 41: Conversations with trees** (page 122)
- **WAY 43: Poetry medicine** (page 128)
- **WAY 44: Poetry prescription** (page 130)

43 Poetry medicine

'It is, to paraphrase William Wordsworth, one person's inside speaking to another's and so it provides the intimate contact we need for healing and for growth for knowing what is human in our lives.' Sheila Bender, 1995 (writer)

When was the last time you wrote or even read a poem of your own? After completing university in 1984, I lost all connection to my interior world. It was in the middle of a weekend retreat in 1985 that I made a dramatic inner reconnection. Suddenly poems started pouring out of me, seemingly from nowhere. I had stuffed so much down inside myself that poetry became the escape route for my emotions and feelings, which spilled out onto the page. On the topic of poetry, Sigmund Freud said, *'Not I, but the poet discovered the unconscious'* (Mayfield & Opher, 2012).

Poetry reduces stress, improves mood and can contribute to a good night's sleep; much research has been carried out to confirm poetry's therapeutic benefits.

In 1994, Dr Robin Philipp from the Department of Social Medicine at the University of Bristol wrote a letter to the *British Medical Journal*, asking about the benefits of reading and writing poetry (Fursland, 1996). Dr Philipp received over 300 replies from health professionals and members of the public. Over half of those who replied said that writing poetry helped to provide a useful outlet for their emotions. Another 42 per cent of the respondents indicated that they identified and gained value from being able to identify with the themes of the poem.

GP's surgeries and health settings across the UK are reporting success when using poetry with their patients. This was highlighted in articles in the *Journal of Holistic Health Care* on the inclusion of poetry in health care settings, indicating significant results including a reduction in consultations and a significant drop in hospital admissions (Mayfield & Opher, 2012).

Consider poems as medicine for your words or pen on those days when you are feeling emotionally spent or even a little bit blue. Sometimes we're afraid of where a poem might take us. It's at these moments that the medicine – some would call it the healing verse of the poem – kicks in, and writing or reading a poem can be a safer way to express your emotions. Poems provide a safe enough distance from strong emotions; contained in a poem they feel safe enough to offload.

SEE ALSO

- **WAY 40: Writing with nature** (page 118)
- **WAY 41: Conversations with trees** (page 122)
- **WAY 44: Poetry prescription** (page 130)

A poem within borders

Think about a difficult or emotional time in your life. Quick-think ten words that spring to mind about the experience. Now write a poem inside the box below, including the ten words you've just listed. The only requirement is you write your poem within the borders of the box. There is no need to edit what you've written.

If you feel stuck, take a leaf out of the book, *Writing Down The Bones* by Natalie

Goldberg (1986): *'Take a poetry book, open to any page, grab a line, write it down and continue from there... every time you get stuck just rewrite your first line and keep going'.* You'll be joining the ranks of writers like Janet Fitch (2006), who always reads *'poetry before I write, to sensitise me to the rhythms and music of language'.*

Write now

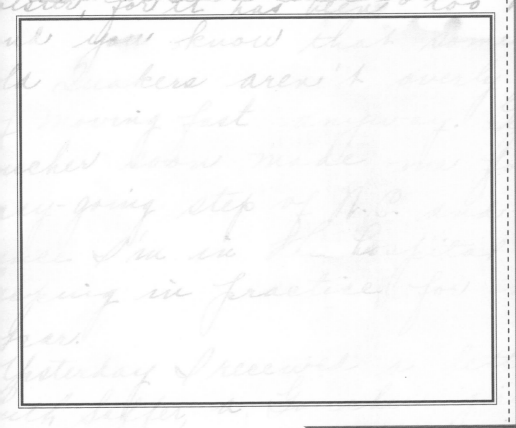

44 Poetry prescription

'Some of my worst wounds/have healed into poems/A few well placed stabs in the back/have released a singing/ trapped between my shoulders.'
Lorna Goodison (Jamaican poet) (McCarthy, 2001)

Writing your own poems is not the only way you can gain therapeutic value from poetry. Let's start by seeing whether there is a poem you can remember from childhood, which resonated for you. Embodying someone else's poem and exploring your feelings and reflections about it has its own therapeutic values and benefits.

In a deeply moving narrative outlined in her book, *Saved By A Poem: The transformative power of words*, Kim Rosen (2011) describes how she embraced learning and getting to know a poem: '*It came when I discovered that taking a poem I loved deeply into my life and speaking it aloud caused a profound integration of every aspect of me, physical, mental and spiritual*'. Rosen advocates a more robust engagement with the poems you love, a view supported by American poet Mary Oliver. Both believe that the need to understand the poem from an analytical stance is secondary. Instead, Oliver says, '*Don't ask what the poem is about. Ask yourself, how does it make you feel*' (Rosen, 2011).

You can of course take this idea one step further and do as I did recently, which was to learn a poem by heart. The poem I chose to learn was *I Go Among Trees* by Wendell Berry (1987). Since learning it my heart I find myself silently reciting it on and off throughout my days. Two lines are deeply etched into my psyche: '*My tasks lie in their places/Where I left them, asleep like cattle*'. These two lines have become a gentle inquiry for me over the last six months.

The lines that resonate with you will be different to the lines that resonate for someone else. Such are the reaching, healing qualities of a poem.

At the end of a hard day at work, instead of reaching for a glass of wine or becoming a couch potato, how about reaching out for a poem? '*Poetry gives us what we want, on the good days, and what we need on the bad*', explains author Amy Bloom (2006).

There are many ways to engage with poetry. You could:
- read a poem aloud to yourself several times
- read a poem to a loved one or a child
- send someone a poetry text or a leave a poem on their voicemail
- leave a poem as your voicemail message
- spend 30 minutes writing a poem of your own
- go to www.daisygoodwin.co.uk/poetry/ poetry-doctor to receive a poem as a prescription for your mood.

SEE ALSO
- **WAY 40: Writing with nature** (page 118)
- **WAY 41: Conversations with trees** (page 122)
- **WAY 42: Walking and writing** (page 126)

Adopt a poem to learn by heart

Set yourself a 28-day challenge of learning a poem – either your own or someone else's – by heart. You will find poems galore at www.poetryarchive.org where you can hear poets reading their own poems. Record yourself on audio or video, reciting your poem. Play it on and off during your week. Send it to a friend or family member as a way of saying hello. Write about the process of learning the poem off by heart in your journal or notebook. What were the different stages like? What meaning are you taking from the poem?

Write now

Tip: Having poems to hand is always helpful. I recommend the following poetry books as a good place to start but there are thousands on the market for you to choose from:

- *Saved By A Poem* by Kim Rosen (2011)
- *Ten Poems To Change Your Life* by Roger Housden (2003)
- *The Gift: Poems by Hafiz the Great Sufi Master* by Hafiz (1999)
- *The Love Poems of Rumi* by Dr Deepak Chopra (1998)
- *101 Poems That Could Save Your Life* by Daisy Goodwin (2002)

WAY 45 Our bodies, our selves

'The body has other ways of talking to us too, it's as elemental as nature itself, like the look and feel of skin. You need only to listen.'
Ayurvedic brochure (Aveda, 2009)

It's easy to forget how relevant the body is to the writing experience. It is the most precious instrument a writer has. Your skin, your cells, are vessels, containers of your memories. Consider the body as a large house or museum where all your stories are stored for safekeeping. We have many stories inside us, waiting to be released. Many of my parent's generation emigrated to the UK or the Americas in the 1950s and 1960s and have held tightly to their stories of grief, betrayal and disappointment. It has taken its toll in many ways, physically and energetically. My own generation has had more success in releasing – or should I say unleashing – many of these stories but there is still more work to be done across all generations and all cultures.

To really work with these stories, to dive deep into our interior world, requires first a relationship with our bodies and a willingness to be still. Breath is the bridge that connects us to the body, to the writer on the page.

Try this breath writing exercise. Settle down and take three long, deep breaths. Now, continue breathing and each time you exhale, write down, as quickly as you can, any words that come into your thoughts as you release the breath. Have no expectations of what you will write – just see what comes. Observing your breath in this way deepens you into your body and into the writing. Make poems from your words. Use the words that are released on the exhale as writing prompts. Enjoy the energy that is released through the fall and the rise of the breath.

As you become more practiced, hold the space between the inhale and the exhale. Imagine your breath plunging deeper into the body to retrieve memories and stories in that sacred space between the exhale and inhale.

One of my deepest relational times with my body was around the age of 38 when I developed a passion for long distance running. I was deeply depressed at the time and began running to ward off the deep hole I was sinking into. I was soon notching up ten miles or more a day. Running became a ritual, a time of deep connection to my body, to nature and, interestingly enough, to my writing. During that period of my life I wrote more than I ever had before, filling reams and reams of notebooks, spilling and exposing myself page after page. Running connected me to my body and the connection to my body deepened me into my writing and retrieving many of my life stories.

In *Writing Begins With The Breath*, Laraine Herring (2007) writes: *'Deep writing comes from our bodies, from our breath and from our ability to remain solid in the places that scare us. It comes from merging with what we are writing – from dissolving our egos so that the real work can emerge through us, without our conditions for success attached to it.'*

SEE ALSO
• **WAY 10: Stilling the mind to write** (page 42)

'I remember...'

Over 10 years ago, in a book by Gregg Levoy called *Callings: Finding and following an authentic life* (1996), I came across the following: '*The writer, Toni Morrison once described how the Mississippi River had been straightened out in places to make room for houses and liveable acreage, and how occasionally the river will flood those places. Flood is the word they use. She said, "but in fact it is not flooding; it is remembering. Remembering where it used to be. All water has a perfect memory and is forever trying to get back to where it was".*' These words by Toni Morrison were one of those quotes that jumped up off the page and grabbed me by the throat. Over the years I have referred to it time and time again as a way of reminding me of the many memories and stories stored in the body. Up to 70 per cent of your body is water. The body may push aside many of your stories and memories but, just like water, the body does not forget. Give it attention and awareness, and the body remembers.

Begin by doing the alternate nostril breathing practice in **WAY 10: Stilling the mind to write** (page 42), followed by your chosen writing ritual. Settle into the moment.

At the top of a blank page in your notebook or journal, write the words, '*I remember...*'. Continue taking deep breaths and wait... keep breathing, keep waiting and listen. Don't give in, wait, breathe and when you hear the rising of words, images, sense of, feel of, in whatever form it arrives, slowly pick up your pen and write.

When it all feels spent, pause, consciously breathe, write '*I remember...*', wait, listen, hear and write.

Write now

46 Body stories

'Write your self, your body must be heard.'
Helene Cixous (professor, philosopher and feminist writer) (Brandeis, 2002)

The body is an intricate and complex living organism that communicates with the senses at different levels. It is through the body that we sense the world, and we speak, write and feel through the labyrinth of the senses. Noticing and tuning into the frequency and vibrations and rhythms of your body will guide you to where your pen wants you to go, to the stories that are waiting to be told. Writing through your body will open you to a wealth of your own lived experiences. The body is an arsenal of untold stories, memories and experiences waiting for you to tap into. Without the body, the container of our stories, what would we write?

The feet are known as the ships of the soul and the eyes the windows of the soul; intuition* is referred to as the third eye. The body is an exquisite communication system, particularly through its complex use of non-verbal body language. We learn and know more about ourselves through what is *not* said than through what *is* said. You will find more currency when you write in your journal when you connect with your body and capture what is going on the page.

SEE ALSO
• **WAY 45: Our bodies, ourselves** (page 132)

Slowly read the following quote from *Visual Medicine: The art of the unknown* by painter and writer Suzette Clough (2012), shared with permission:

'Your body is the root of all creative work. When you paint or write with the whole of yourself, you are in touch with the universe inside your body: everything you have ever felt, heard, seen, or thought – and is yet to become – exists inside you. Your skin, your bones, your breath, your liver, your heart, your hands, your sense of hearing, your eyes, the soft tissue inside your throat, the taste buds on the tongue, the barely audible sighs of the muscles inside the gut, are all resonating chambers for communication and therefore expression. By developing a deep-listening connection to your body mind it becomes possible to create paintings and words, which convey a true experience of communication. They become clear energetic templates of your conversations unfolding with yourself. Learning to use your body as the ground or originating place of your self-connection and expression, embodying your imagination as a muscle, helps to grow the innately healing and physical nature of your creativity.'

Take as long as you need to think and reflect, and then write about your thoughts and reflections about the above quote. Did you notice how your body responded as your eyes moved from word to word, line to line? How did your body receive the quote?

A journey through the senses

The body is your sensory portal and through it, by awakening your senses, you also awaken to life. Explore the body through a journey through the senses. Enjoy this list of sensory writing prompts. Don't try and work through all these prompts in one sitting – use them over the next few weeks, maybe focusing on one particular prompt for two or three days at a time.

Touch

- Who and what have your hands touched in the last seven days?
- Touch five things in the room or space you are in and write about how each item, surface or object feels.

Sight

- Write about a sight worth remembering.
- Write about a sight worth forgetting.
- Close your eyes. When you open them again, touch three subjects in the room or space you are seated in. Write about the feel and texture of each of the objects you touch. How does each feel across the tips of your fingertips, your face, against your arms?
- Close your eyes for five minutes. When you open them again, what do you see, really see around you? Don't just write about the obvious. How does the light hit the computer screen? What names would you give to the different shades of green of the trees from your window?

Sound

- Close your eyes and sit quietly for five minutes. Focus your energy on the sounds in the room. What do you hear? Next, focus on the sounds in your body. Can you hear the soft, almost whispering swish of your blood? The gurgling of lost air trapped in your stomach, the pulse beat of your heart?

Write about the sounds you hear in this moment.
- What are the sounds you remember from your childhood?

Intuition

- Describe three examples from the past when your intuition* was correct. Write about a time when you didn't listen to your intuition*. What happened? What have you learned from the experience? What are you noticing about your relationship with intuition*?

Scent

- Take a moment and consider the smell of the room and the space you are in. What are your body smells? Are you freshly showered, smelling of peppermint? Or can you smell sweaty armpits and garlic breath?
- What scents stimulate past memories for you?

Taste

- Describe the tastes of the last meal you had. What tastes would you choose for your last meal ever?

Voice

- Everyone has a different writing voice. Voices are as unique as the shape and size of our lips, ears and eyes. How well do you really know the sound of your own voice? How would you describe the sound of your voice to a deaf person? Listen to and write about the sound of people's voices as you go through your day. What words would you use to describe the different tones and pitches of the voices you hear? Shrill, expansive, tremoring, hollow, plunging? Do you have different voices depending on the person or the situation you are with?

Write now

WAY 47 Gratitude journal

'Let us be grateful to people who make us happy; they are the charming gardeners who make our souls blossom.'
Marcel Proust (French novelist)

Feeling low? Then dive into the practice of keeping a gratitude journal. Why? Because it does more than just make you feel good. The idea of a gratitude journal was popularised back in the 1990s through the work of Sarah Ban Breathnach, in her book *Simple Abundance (1995)*, along with Oprah Winfrey's passion for the idea.

According to researcher Robert Emmons, author of the book, *Thanks! How the new science of gratitude can make you happier*, (cited in Trespicio, 2008), regular practice of gratitude can have a tremendous impact on your health, and your ability to build relationships and make progress towards personal and professional goals. You even sleep more peacefully.

One way to get into the practice of writing down the things you appreciate and are grateful for is to start a gratitude journal or gratitude pages in your journal or notebook. It's preferable to get a new notebook for this as it stops your entries getting lost amongst all the other things on the page. Being able to see your gratitude list clearly in front of you helps to boost your mood and sense of well-being. Finding and bringing your awareness to the things you are grateful for also helps to change and shift your perspective.

These benefits were further confirmed by a study (Trespicio, 2008) in which one group kept a weekly journal noting up to five things they were grateful about, a second group recorded challenges and hassles and a third wrote about events that affected them. After nine weeks, the first group felt better about their lives and more optimistic about the future than the others; and more than that, they showed fewer physical symptoms and spent more time exercising.

So imagine you've got to the end of a stressful day. There have been a few bumps along the way and all you can think about is throwing yourself into bed. Instead, grab your journal or notebook and lay it out at the side of the bed or next to where you are sitting. Close your eyes and imagine yourself walking back through your day from the moment your eyes popped open to now. Imagine walking through your day with an instrument that resembles a metal detector. What's different about this detector is that it's programmed to pick up the good stuff, no matter how tiny or seemingly insignificant from your day. It will scan and pull to your attention even the most minute details from your day, pulling them into full view so you can appreciate and be grateful for them. You will notice the abundance in your day rather than merely the defects. Tune in to how and when your mood shifts, and how, by engaging with your gratitude, you've gained a new and more flourishing perspective on your day.

SEE ALSO
• **WAY 1: Journal writing and notebooks** (page 20)

Homing in on the good stuff

At the start or end of your day, make a list of five things from the day that you are grateful for. It could be a success at work, getting a hug from your child or something as small as stopping to admire a cluster of flowers in someone's garden. Writing your gratitudes on a regular basis is essential. Writing them down means you are more likely to remember the good stuff. Training yourself in this way will also have you on the constant lookout for the good stuff, no matter how minor it may seem.

Monotony and boredom are often the culprits that cause you to break the pattern of your daily gratitude practice. This is why finding different ways to write your gratitudes can be a resourceful way of not getting bored with embedding this practice.

Five ways to be creatively grateful:

1. Write five people from your life a thank you card. Write one card a day, thanking the person for something they did for you or appreciating a quality or characteristic they have. On the sixth day, write a thank you card to yourself from your inner wise writing self*.

2. For one day, set your alarm on your mobile phone to go off on the hour, every hour. Stop whatever you are doing and write down something or someone you are grateful for.

3. Over a period of one week, leave anonymous thank you cards with people you come into contact with in formal and informal settings. Write the cards beforehand, then add that personal touch and leave them discreetly without being discovered.

4. When you are finding yourself irritated or annoyed with someone, try looking for what Jack Kornfield calls their 'inner nobility' (Trespicio, 2008). If you step back for a moment, what goodness can you see through their actions and intentions? Relate to the individual from this place.

5. We often focus our gratitude on others. Imagine a dear friend writing you a gratitude letter. In it they specifically outline all the things about you they are grateful for. Write the letter from their perspective and then read it aloud to yourself.

Write now

WAY 48 A letter to you

'Such a sweet gift a letter – a piece of handmade writing, in an envelope that is not a bill, sitting in our friend's path when she trudges home from a long day spent among wahoos and savages, a day our words will help repair.'
Garrison Keillor, 1989 (writer)

When was the last time you wrote someone a letter? Or received a handwritten letter in the post, personally addressed to you from a friend or a loved one? It is heartfelt to write a letter using a pen, connecting the hand to the heart. You touch the pen, the pen touches the paper, you touch the envelope, you walk to the letterbox, the person receives it by touch. And in most cases will be touched by your words. Touch is integral to the ritual of writing a letter. I wish I had kept the airmail letters I received from my cousins in the Caribbean in the 1970s. I have fond memories of my mum and dad dictating to me what to write in the letters and me scribing in my best handwriting, retelling stories of how we were all doing.

Letters survive time. Emails and texts are very much of the here and now. Anne Frank, who kept a diary until the age of 15 when she and her family were taken to the Nazi concentration camps, wrote her entries in the forms of letters to a fictional friend she called Kitty.

You can write letters to almost anyone. Perhaps there is something you want to communicate to someone but you are having problems plucking up the courage to do so. Writing it down in a letter allows you the space to say things you might find difficult to say in person. Or write a letter that you don't send, to communicate your feelings or bring about closure to the issue. Whether you send the letter or not doesn't really matter. There will be value in writing the letter so you can gain clarity and release toxic emotions. But your letter writing can also include writing letters to yourself.

Writing letters to the self carries many therapeutic benefits. It will help you make the distinction between events that have happened and your understanding of these events. The process of letter writing helps you to process your thoughts, feelings and emotions from the past and present and to forward your thoughts into the future. It can provide a record of what you have come through and overcome. You have already learned about the many benefits writing by hand holds for you so rekindling one of the oldest forms of written communication can be a cathartic and comforting process.

SEE ALSO
- **WAY 1: Journal writing and notebooks** (page 20)
- **WAY 10: Stilling the mind to write** (page 42)
- **WAY 47: Gratitude journal** (page 136)

Letter to a younger you

Let's begin by writing a letter to a younger you. What memories do you have of yourself as a teenager? Can you recall one of your favourite outfits? What pop stars did you adore and did you have images of them plastered all over your walls? Perhaps you have a favourite image of yourself that brings back memories of this younger you.

Perhaps your memories are of a less secure and confident you. You can see it in the way you held yourself or the way you spoke. What do you wish you could tell your younger self in a letter? Take a minute to think about the younger you between the ages of 14 and 20. Beside you is a writing set including paper, envelopes and a packet of first class stamps. What would you like to write and say to your younger self? What can she not see about her strength and beauty that you would like to bring to her attention? Can you see a life experience event that may cause her pain? What words could you share that will gently tell her that she will be okay and that she will make it through?

Letter to your present self

If you are one of the many blessed women born and still alive on the Caribbean island of Dominica, then you may well be given the opportunity to live to the ripe old age of 100 – Dominica has a high proportion of women centenarians.

Imagine yourself at the age of 100. You are sitting in your favourite spot looking back through albums of your earlier life. Next to you are writing paper, a pen, envelopes and a first class stamp.

As your 100-year-old self, close your eyes and imagine yourself at the age you are now. What have your 100 years alive taught you? What wisdom do you have for the younger you? What suggestions will you share in a letter to you at the age you are right now?

Letter writing prompts

Extend your letter writing to others. Before you pen your letters, sit quietly for a few minutes and meditate on the person you want to write to.

- Instead of sending birthday cards, how about writing your friends and family personalised birthday letters?

- Write a letter to someone you're upset with. Put it aside for a couple of days before you decide whether you will send it or not.

- Write a letter to someone you admire, letting them know what you appreciate and value about them, and send it.

WAY 49 Writing totem

Everyone must leave something behind when he dies, my grandfather said. A child or a book or a painting or a house or a wall built or a pair of shoes made. Or a garden planted. Something your hand touched some way so your soul has somewhere to go when you die, and when people look at that tree or that flower you planted, you're there.'
Ray Bradbury, 2008 (author, in his novel *Fahrenheit 451*)

I hope you have been on a rewarding journey and that you have found something of value here that will inspire you to use writing as a therapeutic tool.

On the right are two luggage tags symbolising the writing journey you have been on in the pages of your journal. On, one describe how you arrived at the start of this journey when you first began using this book. How were you feeling? What were your hopes and expectations? What were your doubts and concerns? On the other, describe where you are now. What's different? What are you returning home with? How has writing supported you? What are you taking with you? Keep these tags as mementos of your write yourself well journey.

Well, we've finally arrived at the end of our time together but hopefully this won't be the end of your time with your pen, notebook or journal. I hope that by being in relationship with this book you'll have cultivated, reinstated or revitalised a new or previously existing relationship with journaling and writing. By nurturing and sustaining this relationship, your writing will continue to serve you and surprise you. According to neuroscientist and medical doctor Dr Tara Swart (2012), *'Anything that releases emotions from your brain and body – like aerobic exercise, psychological therapies or journaling – reduces stress levels and guides the path to emotional stability and recovery'*. We now have a body of research that confirms that, in the right context, journaling and writing help to stabilise emotions and in many instances lead to creative and emotional recovery.

SEE ALSO
- **WAY 6: Writing habits and rituals** (page 32)
- **WAY 9: Inner wise writing self** (page 40)
- **WAY 47: Gratitude journal** (page 136)
- **WAY 48: A letter to you** (page 138)

An example of framing and celebrating your writing, from one of our writing retreat members, Jen Morgan. Printed with permission, © Jen Morgan 2012. The painting in the background is an example of visual medicine artwork produced by psychotherapist and painter Suzette Clough.

A special writing ritual for you

You now have a body of work, your written responses and reflections gathered through the various 'Write now' practices, which I hope have offered you many connections to your own wisdom, insights and healing. It can be so easy to slip into what psychologists call the paradise syndrome*, where once we achieve one goal we're off in hot pursuit of the next one without having really savoured what we have just achieved. You can avoid this by getting creative and creating something symbolic that honours your writing journey. You will need to set aside an hour for this final practice. Before you begin, activate a state of mindfulness* by performing the alternate nostril breathing practice from **WAY 10: Stilling the mind to write** (page 42) and your preferred writing ritual.

No need to rush this one. Begin by leafing through your notebook or journal. As you move through the pages, be on the lookout for a piece of your writing that jumps out at you, is meaningful to you or you feel a sense of pride about. Make it no more than three or four lines. It could be a few sentences from one of the free writes or morning pages practices, a response to one of the 'Write now' practices or a message or letter from your inner wise writing self. Imagine you had to choose one example of a small slice of your writing – which one would you select?

Once you have decided on the words you will be honouring, either tear or cut out the words from your notebook or rewrite them on quality card or luxury paper. To honour your journey, you are now going to frame your writing as a memento of your experience. You can purchase inexpensive frames from local shops or supermarkets. Your writing will bring any frame you use alive. Get creative. Paint or colour your card or paper, or use luggage tags like we did on page 41. Shown opposite is an example of a framed piece of writing done by one of our writing retreat group members during a series of rituals we did to create writing totems to celebrate each person's writing.

Find a sacred location in your home where your framed work will serve as a reminder of the value and gifts journaling and writing has given and has to give to you. Alternatively, take a photo of your writing totem on your phone and view it regularly. Or print a photo of your framed writing and stick it into your journal or notebook. Take a moment to really take in what you have created. You might even want to spend a few minutes free writing in your journal or write a poem to honour your journey.

I leave you with these words from the mystical Persian poet Rumi: '*Don't be satisfied with the stories, how things have gone with others. Unfold your own myth, without complicated explanation, so everyone will understand the passage. We have opened you*' (Mabey, 2008).

Always write your words from your heart to the page – they will serve you well. I wish you a continuous flow of blessings on your continued journey to write yourself well.

GLOSSARY

Alpha state

A state of mind where you are calm and relaxed, receptive to new information and knowledge and more resourceful.

Appreciative inquiry

A management and organisational development approach pioneered by David Cooperrider and Suresh Srivastva, which focuses on what's going well in an organisation rather than what isn't and building on strengths and potentials.

Free association

A psychoanalytical technique developed by Sigmund Freud, the founder of psychoanalysis, which promotes spontaneous, logically unconstrained and undirected association of ideas, emotions, and feelings.

Functional fixedness

The tendency to perceive an object only for its common usage (the idea was first articulated in the 1930s by Karl Duncker), for example, seeing a pen only as usable for writing when it could be used for tying your hair into a bun, opening letters or as a bookmark. Getting out of a functional fixedness mindset can help you to become a better problem solver.

Hebbs Law

States that 'neurons that fire together wire together'. Canadian psychologist Donald Hebb came up with Hebbs Law in 1949 and was influential in showing how neurons contribute to psychological processes and learning.

Inner child

A concept used in popular and analytical psychology, describing the part of the adult self that remains childlike.

Inner critic

A concept used in popular psychology to refer to a person's inner voice that judges and demeans them, telling them they are bad, wrong, inadequate, worthless, guilty and so on.

Inner wise writing self

The part of the self that embodies all that is right and positive and affirming of who you are. Part writing coach, part mentor, part inner wise woman/man.

Intuition

Sometimes called the sixth of the core senses. Gives us the ability to know something directly without analytic reasoning. Intuition bridges the gap between the conscious and unconscious parts of our mind, between instinct and reason and between the left and the right brains.

Karpman Drama Triangle

A model created by psychotherapist Stephen Karpman, outlining dysfunctional social interactions. Each position on the triangle (victim, rescuer and persecutor) represents a common and ineffective response to conflict, more likely to embed disharmony than resolve it.

Life script

Originated from Eric Berne founder of transactional analysis (TA) in the 1950s. Berne's hypothesis is that people form a 'script' that is essentially their beliefs about who they are, what the world is like, how they relate to the world, how the world relates to them and how others treat them.

Mindfulness

A technique for turning off busy thoughts, derived from Buddhist meditation practices, involving focusing awareness on moment-by-moment experience, for example focusing on the breath entering and leaving the nose. It involves consciously bringing awareness to your here-and-now experience with openness, interest and receptiveness. Mindfulness means paying attention in a particular way, on purpose and non-judgementally, in the present moment.

Morning pages

A creative recovery tool devised by Julia Cameron. They consist of three daily pages of uncensored thoughts written in longhand first thing in the day, in a notebook or journal. Morning pages are private, personal notes and not to be shared with others.

Narrative therapy

A form of psychotherapy using narrative, developed during the 1970s and 1980s, largely by Australian psychotherapist Michael White and New Zealander David Epston. Sometimes known as 're-authoring' or 're-storying' conversations.

Neuroplasticity

The science of physical brain changes and the knowledge that the brain has the potential to 'rewire' itself and form new neural pathways even in old age.

Neuroscience

The scientific study of the nervous system, how the brain works and the network of sensory nerve cells (neurons) throughout the body.

Non-dominant hand

The hand you don't normally write with. Your dominant hand is connected to your conscious, thinking side, and your non-dominant hand is connected to your intuitive, feeling, creative side.

Paradise syndrome

A psychological condition in which, despite achieving their goals and dreams, an individual is still left feeling dissatisfied.

Perceptual positions

A neuro-linguistic programming (NLP) model, originally formulated by John Grinder and Judith DeLozier in 1987, for developing empathy in situations of conflict.

Reticular activating system (RAS)

The part of the brain responsible for sleep, respiratory responses, motor and motivation. It receives input from the senses and filters those inputs to allow through only information that is important to you.

Shadow

A term developed by psychiatrist Carl Jung to refer to the entirety of the unconscious, ie. everything of which a person is not fully conscious. Because we tend to reject or remain ignorant of the least desirable aspects of our personality, the shadow is largely negative.

TED Triangle

Stands for The Empowerment Dynamic. Created by executive coach David Emerald as an alternative to the positions on the Karpman Drama Triangle.

Transactional analysis (TA)

A therapeutic approach developed by Canadian psychoanalyst, and psychiatrist Eric Berne in the 1960s and 1970s. Berne mapped interpersonal relationships and identified three ego states: the parent, the adult and the child.

USEFUL RESOURCES

Writing prescriptions: 49 books I personally recommend for your write yourself well journey

On writing

Ballon R (2007) *The Writer's Portable Therapist: 25 sessions to a creativity cure*. Avon, Mass: Adams Media.

Brandeis G (2002) F*ruitflesh: Seeds of inspiration for women who write*. New York: Harper Collins.

Cameron J (1982) *The Artist's Way*. London: Pan Books.

Cameron J (1998) *The Right to Write*. New York: Putnam.

Cameron J (1992) *Walking in this World*. London: Rider.

Cameron J (2004) *The Sound of Paper*. New York: Penguin.

Dilliard A (1989) *The Writing Life*. New York: Harper & Row.

Friedeman B (1994) Writing Past Dark. New York: Harper Perennial.

Goldberg N (1986) *Wild Mind*. London: Rider.

Goldberg N (1986) *Writing Down The Bones*. Boston: MASS: Shambhala Publications Inc.

Gray DR (1998) *Soul Between the Lines*. New York: Avon Brooks.

Herring L (2007) *Writing Begins With The Breath: Embodying Your Authentic Voice*. Boston, MASS: Shamhbala Publications Inc, USA.

Holzer BN (1994) *A Walk Between Heaven and Earth*. New York: Bell Tower.

Hooks B (1999) *Remembered Rapture*. London: The Women's Press.

Lamott A (1995) *Bird by Bird*. New York: Anchor Books.

Louden J (1999) *The Women's Retreat Guide*. San Francisco: Harper.

Maisel E (1999) *Deep Writing: 7 principles that bring ideas to life*. New York: Jeremy P. Tarcher/Putnam.

Peterson KE (2008) *The Write Type: Discover your true writer's identity and create a customized writing plan*. MA: Adams Media.

Reeves J (1999) *A Writer's Book Of Days: A spirited companion and lively muse for the writing life*. Novato, CA: New World Library.

Reeves J (2002) *Writing Alone, Writing Together*. Novato, CA: New World Library.

Reeves J (2005) *The Writer's Retreat Kit*. Novato, CA: New World Library.

SARK (2008) *Juicy Pens, Thirsty Paper*. New York: Three Rivers Press.

Sarton M (1992) *Journal of a Solitude*. WW Norton & Co.

Sellers H (2005) *Page by Page*. Cincinnati: Writer's Digest Books.

Sellers H (2007) *Chapter after Chapter*. Cincinnati: Writer's Digest Books.

Sher G (1999) *One Continuous Mistake: Four noble truths for writers*. New York: Penguin.

Poetry

Gibran K (1923) *The Prophet*. New York: Alfred A Knopf.

Goodison L (1993) S*elected Poems*. Michigan: University of Michigan.

Goodwin D (1980) *101 Poems To Get You Through The Day and Night*. London: Harper Collins.

Goodwin D (1980) *101 Poems To Keep You Sane*. London: Harper Collins.

Haviz (1999) *The Gift – Poems by Hafiz the Great Sufi Master*. Translated by Daniel Ladinsky. New York: Penguin Putnam.

Housden R (2003) *Ten Poems to Change Your Life*. London: Hodden Mobius.

Mabey J (2008) Rumi: *A spiritual treasury*. One World Publications.

Rosen K (2011) *Saved by a Poem: The transformative power of words*. California: Hay House.

Wooldridge SG (1996) *Poemcrazy: Freeing your life with words*. New York: Three Rivers Press.

Nature
Blackwell L (2009) *The Life and Love Of Trees*. San Francisco: Chronicle Books.

Kindred G (2005) *Earth Wisdom*.California: Hay House.

Kindred G (2005) *Sacred Celebrations*.Somerset: Gothic Images.

Pakenham T (1996) *Meetings with Remarkable Trees*. London: Cassell.

Pakenham T (2002) *Remarkable Trees of the World*. London: Cassell.

Pakenham T (2004) *The Remarkable Baobab Tree*. London: Weidenfeld & Nicholson.

Paterson JM (1996) *Tree Wisdom: The definitive guidebook to the myth, folklore and healing powers of trees*. London: Thorsons.

Pollet C (2010) *Bark: An intimate look at the world's trees*. London: Francis Lincoln.

Shamir I (1999) *Advice From A Tree*. Colorado: Better World Press.

Shamir I (1999) *Poet Tree: The Wilderness I Am*. Colorado: Better World Press.

Tudge C (2005) *The Secret Life Of Trees: How they live and why they matter*. London: Penguin Books Ltd.

Others
Conway S (2012) *This I Know For Sure*. Guilford, CT: Skirt.

Harris R (2000) *20-Minute Retreats*. London: Pan.

Wall S (2011) *Quiet London*. London: Francis Lincoln.

Articles and online resources
Gillie Bolton's website: www.gilliebolton.com

Article, *Not-Knowing*, adapted from a talk by Gil Fronsdal: www.insightmeditationcenter.org/books-articles/articles/not-knowing

Article, *The Free Fall Method of Creative Writing*, by Samantha Garner: http://suite101.com/article/the-free-fall-method-of-creative-writing-a102047

Article, *Why much of recent neuroscience research is a waste of money*, by Elisha Goldstein: http://blogs.psychcentral.com/mindfulness/2010/07/why-recent-neuroscience-research-is-a-waste-of-money

Mari L McCarthy's *CreateWriteNow* personal journal blog: www.createwritenow.com/personal-journal-blog/bid/87523/Journal-Writing-Rewrites-Your-Money-Script

Jackie Morris's website: www.jackiemorris.co.uk

Article, *Keeping a Diary Makes you Happier*, by Ian Sample: www.guardian.co.uk science/2009/feb/15/psychology-usa

REFERENCES

Adrian C (2007) *Oprah Magazine*, May, p305.

Alcott LM (2005) *Little Women, Little Men and Jo's Boys*. New York: Literary Classics of the United States, Inc.

Armstrong K (2008) *The Circles: A guide to mapping out your heart's true feelings*. New York: Atria Books.

Aronie NS (1998) *Writing from the Heart: Tapping the power of your inner voice*. New York: Hyperion.

Aveda (2009) *30 Years On*. Promotional brochure.

Ballon R (2007) *The Writer's Portable Therapist: 25 sessions to a creativity cure*. Avon, MASS: Adams Media.

Bane R (2012) *Around The Writer's Block: Using Brain Science to Solve Writer's Resistance*. New York: Tarcher/Penguin.

Bender S (1995) *Writing Personal Essays: How to shape your life experiences for the page*. Cincinnati, Ohio: Writer's Digest Books.

Bennett-Goleman T (2003) *Emotional Alchemy: How your mind can heal your heart*. London: Rider.

Berry W (1987) *Sabbaths*. New York: North Point Press.

Bloom A (2006) Why poetry can save your life. *Oprah Magazine*, December.

Bolton G (2011) *Write Yourself: Creative writing and personal development*. London:Jessica Kingsley Publishers Ltd.

Bounds G (2010). How handwriting trains the brain. *The Wall Street Journal*, 5 October. Available at http://online.wsj.com/article/SB10001424052748704631504575531932754922518.html (accessed 30 October 2012).

Bradbury R (2008) *Fahrenheit 451*. Flamingo Modern Classics.

Brandeis G (2002) *Fruitflesh: Seeds of inspiration for women who write*. New York: Harper Collins Publishers Inc.

Breathnach S (1995) *Simple Abundance: A daybook of comfort and joy*. New York: Warner Books, Inc.

Bridges W (2004) *Transitions: Making sense of life's changes*. Cambridge, MA: Da Capo Press.

Brown B. (2010) *The Gift Of Imperfection*. Minnesota: Hazelden.

Butler-Bowdon T (2012) The Long Game. *Psychologies*, August.

Cameron J (1982) *The Artist's Way*. London: Pan Books.

Cameron J (1996) *The Vein of Gold: A journey to your creative heart*. London: Pan Books.

Canfield J & Switzer J (2006) *The Success Principles: How to get from where you are to where you want to be*. New York: Harper Collins.

Chopra D & Fereydoun K (1998) *The Love Poems Of Rumi*. New York: Harmony.

Clough, S. (2012) *Visual Medicine*. Visual Medicine Productions.

Connor J (2008) *Writing Down Your Soul: How to activate and listen to the extraordinary voice within*. San Francisco: Conari Press.

Conway S (2012) *This I Know: Notes on unravelling the heart*. Connecticut: Guilford Press.

Covey SR (2004) *The Seven Habits of Highly Effective People*. London: Simon & Schuster UK Ltd.

Davis J (2012) Why writing trumps positive thinking alone for goal setting. *Psychology Today*, 20 February. Available at http://www.psychologytoday.com/blog/tracking-wonder/201202/why-writing-trumps-positive-thinking-alone-goal-setting (accessed 17 December 2012).

Donius WA (2012) *The Thought Revolution: How to unlock your inner genius*. Cleveland, OH: Changing Lives Press.

Edwards B (2008) *The New Drawing on the Right Side of the Brain*. Harper Collins Publishers.

Ekman P (2007) *Emotions Revealed: Recognising faces and feelings to improve communication and emotional life*. New York: Henry Holt & Company, LLC.

Fischer N (2001) *Oprah Magazine*, November, p.45.

Fitch J (2006) Oprah Talks to Janet Fitch. *Oprah Magazine*, September, p.280.

Franck F (1973) *The Zen of Seeing: Seeing/drawing as meditation*. New York: Vantage Books/Random House.

Friedman B (1995) *Writing Past Dark: Envy, fear, distraction and other dilemmas in the writer's life*. New York: Harper Collins Publishers, Inc.

Frost R (1949) *Collected Poems of Robert Frost*. New York: Holt, Rinehart and Winston.

Fursland E (1996) Textual healing. *Here's Health*, August.

Garfield M (2002) Revolutionary Road. *Real Simple* 3(4) 134.

Garner S (2009) *The Free Fall Method of Creative Writing*. Available at http://suite101.com/article/the-free-fall-method-of-creative-writing-a102047 (accessed 26 October 2012).

George M (2011) *1001 Meditations: How to discover peace of mind*. London: Watkins Publishing.

Globus, D (e-book) *3 Rituals: One for gratitude, one for grounding, one for release*.

Goldberg N (1986) *Writing Down The Bones*. Boston, MASS: Shambhala Publications Inc.

Gollwitzer PM (1999) Implementations intentions: strong effects of simple plans. *American Psychologist* 54 (7).

Gollwitzer PM & Brandstatter V (1997) Implementation Intentions and Effective Goal Pursuit. *Journal of Personality and Social Psychology* 73, 186–199.

Good Housekeeping (2008) February edition, p.72.

Goodwin D (2002) *101 Poems That Could Save Your Life*. Harper Collins Publishers.

Gregory D (2006) *The Creative License: Giving yourself permission to be the artist you truly are*. New York: Hyperion.

Guardian (16 November 2010) In praise of the daily walk. Available at www.guardian.co.uk/global/2010/nov/16/in-praise-of-daily-walk/print (accessed 17 December 2012).

Harris N (1999) Off the couch: an introduction to labyrinths and their therapeutic properties. *Annals of the American Psychotherapy Association* (March/April).

Harris R (2001) *Twenty-Minute Retreats: Revive your spirits in just minutes a day*. Pan Books.

Haviz (1999) *The Gift – Poems by Hafiz the Great Sufi Master*. Translated by Daniel Ladinsky. New York: Penguin Putnam.

Hemingway E (1929) *A Farewell To Arms*. Arrow.

Herring L (2007) *Writing Begins With The Breath: Embodying your authentic voice*. Boston, MASS: Shambhala Publications Inc.

Hesse H (1999) *Siddhartha*. Dover Publishing, Inc.

Holden (2012) *Coaching for Success*. Training course.

Housden R (2003) *Ten Poems to Change Your Life*. London: Hodder Mobius.

Hurston ZN (1973) *Their Eyes Were Watching God*. New York: Harper Collins Publishers.

Jacobs B (2004) *Writing For Emotional Balance*. Oakland, CA: New Harbinger Publications, Inc.

Janki D (2010) *Companion of God*. London: Brahma Kumaris Information Services Ltd.

Johnson R (2010) In praise of the daily walk. *Guardian* 16 November. Available at www.guardian.co.uk/global/2010/nov/16/in-praise-of-daily-walk/print (accessed 17 December 2012).

Jung CG, Adler G & Hull RFC (1983) *Alchemical Studies*, Vol 13, paragraph 335 (p265). Princeton, NY: Princeton University Press.

Keillor G (1989) *We Are Still Married*. London: Faber & Faber Ltd.

Kiplinger (2012) Your worst money problems are all in your head. *NASDAQ*, 4 July. Available at www.nasdaq.com/article/your-worst-money-problems-are-all-in-your-head-cm153229#.UMs_Ju2RtoZ (accessed 17 December 2012).

Klauser HA (2001) *Write it Down, Make It Happen*. London: Simon & Schuster.

Levoy G (1996) *Callings: Finding and following an authentic life*. New York: Three Rivers Press.

Liebenguth K (2012) When we are outside new insights emerge. *Psychologies*, May.

Mabey J (2008) *Rumi: A spiritual treasury*. One World Publications.

Maisel E (1999) *Deep Writing: 7 principles that bring ideas to life*. New York: Jeremy P. Tarcher/Putnam.

Mayfield S & Opher S (2012) A Poet in every practice – the value of words in primary care. *Journal of Holistic Health Care* 9 (2).

McCarthy K (2001) *Bittersweet: An anthology of Black women's poetry*. London: The Women's Press.

McCarthy M (2012) Journal writing rewrites your money script. *createwritenow* blog. Available at www.createwritenow.com/personal-journal-blog/bid/87523/Journal-Writing-Rewrites-Your-Money-Script (accessed 17 December 2012).

McGill B (2012) *Voice of Reason: Speaking to the great and good spirit of revolutionary mind*. Sarasota, FL: PaperLyon Publishing Company.

McMeekin G (2000) *12 Secrets of Highly Creative Women: A portable mentor*. San Francisco: Conari Press.

Meek KR (2001) *The Science Of Forgiveness*. Waco, Texas: The Center for Christian Ethics, Baylor University.

Monden A (2012) Walk of life. *UK Coaching At Work* 7 (2).

Morgan A (2000) *What is Narrative Therapy?* London: Dulwich Centre Publications. Available at: www.dulwichcentre.com.au/what-is-narrative-therapy.html (accessed 17 December 2012).

Monroe V (2007) *Oprah Magazine*, March.

Murphy PA (2011) The science of intuition: an eye opening guide to your sixth sense. *Oprah Magazine*, July.

Neustatter A (2012) The Power of words. *Psychologies*, January.

Nin A (1944–47) *The Diary of Anais Nin*. New York & London: Harcourt Brace Jovanovich Publishers.

Noble S (2012) *The Enlightenment Of Work: Revealing the path to happiness, contentment in your job*. London: Watkins Publishing.

O'Connor F (2007) *Oprah Magazine*, May, p.305.

Olalla J (2010) *Coaching At Work*. Conference, London, 2010.

Paterson JM (1996) *Tree Wisdom: The definitive guidebook to the myth, folklore and healing powers of trees*. London: Thorsons.

Pennebaker JW (1997) *Opening Up: The healing power of expressing emotions*. London: Guilford Press.

Pennebaker JW (2012) *The Secret Life Of Pronouns: What our words say about us*. New York: Bloomsbury Press.

Perle L (2006) *Money, A Memoir: Women's emotions and cash*. New York: Henry Holt and Company.

Pickard N & Lott L (2003) *Seven Steps on The Writer's Path: The journey from frustration to fulfillment*. The Random House Publishing Group.

Phillips K (2005) *Transactional Analysis In Organisations*. Cheshire: Keri Phillips Associates.

Pollet C (2010) *Bark: An intimate look at the world's trees*. London: Francis Lincoln.

Post S & Neimark J (2008) *Why Good Things Happen to Good People: How to live a longer, healthier, happier life by the simple act of giving*. New York: Broadway Books.

Rainer T (1978) *The New Diary: How to use a journal for Self Guidance and Expanded Creativity*. Los Angeles: Jeremy. P. Tarcher.

Reeves J (1999) *A Writer's Book Of Days: A spirited companion and lively muse for the writing life*. Novato, CA: New World Library.

Rilke RA (2000) *Letters To A Young Poet*. Novato, CA: New World Library.

Rosen K (2011) *Saved by a Poem: The transformative power of words*. California: Hay House.

Ryan RM (2010) *Science Daily*, 4 June.

Sample I (2009) Keeping a diary makes you happier. *Guardian*, 15 February. Available at www.guardian.co.uk/science/2009/feb/15/psychology-usa (accessed 13 October 2012).

SARK (2008) *Juicy Pens, Thirsty Paper*. New York: Three Rivers Press.

SARK (2012) Writing Tele-class.

Schubert K (2007) *On Narrative Therapy: Re-writing the stories of our lives*. Mental Health Association of Australia. Available at www.mhaca.org.au (accessed 7 December 2012).

Schwartz T (2011) *Be Excellent At Anything: Four changes to get more out of work and life*. London: Simon & Schuster UK Ltd.

Science Daily (2010) *Spending Time in Nature Makes People Feel More Alive*. Available at www.sciencedaily.com/releases/2010/06/100603172219.htm (accessed 17 December 2012).

Selling B (2003) *Writing From Within: A guide to creativity and life story writing*. Barnes and Noble.

Sher G (1999) *One Continuous Mistake: Four noble truths for writers*. London: Penguin Group.

Swart, T. (2012). Author Interview.

Trespicio T (2008) Thank-You Therapy. *Body+Soul Magazine*, September, p130.

Tudge C (2005) *The Secret Life Of Trees: How they live and why they matter*. London: Penguin Books Ltd.

Vogt E, Brown J & Isaacs D (2003) *The Art of Powerful Questions. Catalyzing insight, innovation and action*. Mill Valley, CA: Whole Systems Associates.

Williamson M (1994) *Illuminata: A return to prayer*. USA: Riverhead Books.

Wollenberg A (2011) The Smell of Happiness. *Psychologies Magazine* (August).

Wooldridge SG (1996) *Poemcrazy: Freeing your life with words*. New York: Three Rivers Press.

Yalom ID (2001) *The Gift Of Therapy: Reflections on being a therapist*. Piatkus Books Ltd.

Other titles in the *49 Ways to Well-being Series* include:

49 Ways to Think Yourself Well
49 Ways to Eat Yourself Well
49 Ways to Move Yourself Well
49 Ways to Mental Health Recovery
49 Ways to Sexual Well-being

For more details visit
www.stepbeachpress.co.uk/well-being